THE GOSPEL
IN THE
FEASTS OF ISRAEL

by

VICTOR BUKSBAZEN

THE FRIENDS OF ISRAEL
Gospel Ministry, Inc.

475 White Horse Pike
W. Collingswood, N.J. 08107

Eighth Printing 1976

Published by
The Friends of Israel

Gospel Ministry, Inc.

475 White Horse Pike
W. Collingswood, N.J. 08107

Printed in U.S.A.

Introduction

You have before you the eighth edition of THE GOSPEL IN THE FEASTS OF ISRAEL. Though Dr. Buksbazen wrote this volume in 1954 it is just as fresh and contemporary as if written today. He possessed keen spiritual insight, and *eternal truth is eternally true.*

For centuries a segment of Christendom deliberately sought to disassociate itself from its JUDAIC HERITAGE—as though a son can divorce himself from his mother.

Today the church's disassociation from Judaic culture is not so much deliberate as inculcated. When historic footprints are long and deep, it becomes hard to climb out of them. For the Jew this has often meant that he has not been evangelized with love, nor within a philosophical framework within which he could identify. For the church it has meant far less comprehension of the New Testament Scripture. There is not a single major New Testament doctrine which is not clarified, amplified or illustrated in the Old Testament Scripture.

Most happily, the evangelical church is beginning to see these long-standing failures and is now moving to correct them.

The birth of the modern State of Israel, prophetic implications of present world events, and increased numbers of Jews who are receiving their Messiah have been the catalyst for this change of attitude.

Biblical Christianity is not a continuation of Judaism, but it is the logical outgrowth and consequence of adherence to Moses and the prophets.

THE GOSPEL IN THE FEASTS OF ISRAEL will serve to underscore that intimate relationship. The author of the book addressed "to the Hebrews" saw that relationship when he wrote,

"Looking unto Jesus the author and finisher of our faith . . ." Hebrews 12:12.

If God be pleased, may the searching Jew who picks up this volume find that accepting Jesus as Messiah is not inconsistent with his great heritage, and may the true Christian see anew, or more brilliantly, his eternal indebtedness to the descendants of Abraham through Jacob.

Marvin J. Rosenthal
General Director
The Friends of Israel
Gospel Ministry, Inc.

Foreword

By OSWALD J. SMITH, Litt.D.

As I read "The Gospel in the Feasts of Israel" I was amazed at the author's depth of understanding and the evidence of his penetrating study and spiritual insight. Here we have a true masterpiece which should be read with real profit by all—Jews and Gentiles alike.

Mr. Buksbazen throws an abundance of new light on a number of very difficult problems, and draws on his background of learning in the Holy Scriptures and Jewish lore, to bring out precious truths not always discernible at first sight.

His explanation of the customs and practices, as well as the beliefs of the Jewish people, is most illuminatng and instructive, and his interpretation of Hebrew terms clear and convincing. The author's presentation of the different feasts of Israel will prove most helpful to every student of the Word of God and to every Christian worker.

It has been my privilege to know Mr. Buksbazen for a number of years now and I think of him, first as a missionary, then as a Christian gentleman, and now as an expositor and author. He is interested first and foremost in Jewish evangelization and all that he says and writes has that end in view.

Many will undoubtedly study "The Gospel in the Feasts of Israel" with deep interest and some, I trust, will be brought to the Saviour as a result, for no one can read it without being moved Godward.

I heartily commend it and pray that it will enjoy a widespread distribution, not only in America but throughout the entire world.

Oswald J. Smith

The Peoples Church
Toronto, Ontario, Canada

Contents

Illustrations

Booths of Branches on the House-tops.

Chapter One

Passover and The Lord's Supper

*"Beneath the blood-stained lintel I with my
    children stand;*
*A messenger of evil is passing through
    the land.*
*There is no other refuge from the
    destroyer's face;*
*Beneath the blood-stained lintel shall be our
    hiding-place.*

*"The Lamb of God has suffered, our sins and
    griefs He bore;*
*By faith the blood is sprinkled above our
    dwelling's door.*
*The foe who seeks to enter doth fear that
    sacred sign;*
*Tonight the blood-stained lintel shall shelter
    me and mine."*

JUDAISM and Christianity are as insepara-
ble as seed and flower, or tree and fruit.
Nowhere can the organic relationship between
the two be observed more clearly than in the
Passover of the Jews and the Last Supper
as ordained by our Lord, when He and His
twelve disciples sat around the passover
table.

"Now the first day of the feast of unleavened
bread the disciples came to Jesus, saying to

1

him, Where wilt thou that we prepare for thee to eat the passover?

And he said, Go into the city to such a man, and say unto him, The Master saith, My time is at hand; I will keep the passover at thy house with my disciples.

And the disciples did as Jesus had appointed them; and they made ready the passover"— Matthew 26:17-19.

In the light of the New Testament we obtain a full understanding of the Passover, while the deepest meaning of the Lord's Supper cannot be fathomed without the historic background of the Jewish Passover.

Did the Jews in the times of our Lord celebrate the Passover the same way as they do today? Substantially yes, for the Jews preserve their traditions tenaciously and faithfully.

Passover and Easter Related

Passover and Easter generally coincide in time (usually March or early April). There is however a deeper spiritual interdependence and unity between them. Wherever there is a city with a major Jewish population we may observe the feverish preparations for the Passover—a joyful and solemn occasion, officially designated the "Season of Liberation" and also the "Season of Joy."

The deliverance of Israel from Egypt is the central point in Jewish history and worship, even as Calvary is the central point in the Christian faith. For on Calvary the work of redemption was accomplished for every believer.

Passover Preparations

On the eve before the day of Passover, Jewish homes are cleansed of all leaven, in accordance with the command of the Lord in Exodus 12:15 "Seven days shall ye eat unleavened bread; even the first day ye shall put away leaven out of your houses: for whosoever eateth leavened bread from the first day until the seventh day, that soul shall be cut off from Israel."

Most likely the youngest son has had a hand in helping father perform the Mitzva (a

Baking of Matzos (Unleavened Bread)

3

meritorious deed). Obligingly the little boy probably has scattered a few crumbs in the corners of the house so that father might be able to sweep them away and pronounce the traditional benediction for the occasion.

"Blessed art thou, Lord our God, King of the universe who has sanctified us with thy commandments and commanded us to remove all leaven from our household."

For days and weeks mother would be busy giving the house a thorough spring cleaning, in preparation for that great season of Pesach, the Passover. Also the pots and pans have had to be cleansed in boiling water from all vestige of leaven that might possibly cling to them, before they could be used for the feast of the "Unleavened Bread."

Only then could the "matzos," the unleavened bread, be brought into the home.

In the evening after the service in the synagogue the father returns to a festively decorated home. The family is dressed in holiday finery assembled around the table. Now the father is ready to preside, reclining in kingly manner, and to conduct the celebration. The traditional symbols of the Passover are spread on the table. The house is well lit even as were the Hebrew homes when darkness descended in Egypt.

Elijah—Messiah's Herald

A place of honor is reserved for Elijah, the herald of the Messiah, lest he come on this most solemn night and announce the joyful news that Messiah has at last come, for the rabbis say Messiah is most likely to come on the night of Passover. And so a place at the table is set for Elijah, the traditional cup of Elijah is filled, and an empty chair awaits the heavenly guest. Will he come? Will he sip the wine? These are the secret questions of every heart, especially of the younger still hopeful and trusting generation. What high hopes that cup symbolizes and what dreams are shattered at the sight of its remaining untouched!

Passover Symbols

We observe on the passover table a glass of salt water, symbolic of the Red Sea through which God led His people, and also reminiscent of the tears of the Hebrew ancestors shed during their enslavement.

Also the unleavened bread, or the matzos, three of them, are covered with a white napkin. These matzos are descendants in a straight line from the original unleavened cakes which the Jews hastily prepared when the truculent Pharaoh at last decreed that the Jews leave—immediately.

Prominent among the passover symbols is the shank bone in place of the lamb which God commanded be eaten in every Jewish household on the night of the passover.

"In the tenth day of this month they shall take to them every man a lamb, according to the house of their fathers, a lamb for an house" —Exodus 12.3.

This is the eternal reminder that it was the blood of the lamb, sprinkled on the doorposts of every Jewish home, which stood between them and death on that passover night when God wrought his wrath on the firstborn of Egypt.

The four cups of red wine are symbols of the

5

blood of the lamb, and the hard boiled egg is symbolic of the second sacrifice for the Passover day. The bitter herbs, usually horseradish, bring tears to the eyes of the participants and remind them of the bitterness and the sorrow of the erstwhile slaves of Pharaoh, their own forefathers.

Look at the charoseth. It is a claylike substance made of apples and nuts which typifies the clay from which the Israelites were forced to fashion bricks to build the mighty cities and fortresses of the Pharaohs, Pithom and Raamses.

It was probably at this point that our Saviour washed His hands and girded Himself with a towel and stooped to wash the feet of the disciples.

"He took a towel, and girded himself . . . and began to wash the disciples' feet"—John 13:4,5.

We Were Slaves in Egypt

And now the father washes his hands and pronounces the benediction over the wine and all drink of it, even as our Lord and His disciples did.

Then begins the long recital in a sonorous chanting voice of the story of God's deliverance of His people from Egypt.

"We were slaves of Pharaoh in Egypt". . .

For two hours he relates in detail the events preceding passover, enlarging on every point, for it is a good and meritorious deed to make much of God's mighty exploits. At one point all the symbols on the table are explained. The poor and the hungry are invited to come in and to partake.

When counting the ten plagues which God

sent on Pharaoh and his people, the father dips his finger in the cup, causing one drop of wine to fall for each plague, and counts:

Daam, tsefardea, Kinim—blood, frogs, vermin . . .

Only one thing, the essence of the Passover, is missing—the lamb, ordained to be sacrificed and consumed by every Jewish family. Passover without the lamb is like a wedding without the bride. What the modern Jews celebrate today is not the passover but the Feast of the Unleavened Bread.

Nevertheless the people rejoice, remembering what God did for their ancestors, delivering them from the thraldom of enslavement and making them a new people under God, bringing them into the promised land.

Year by year now for some thirty-five centuries the Jews have been repeating the story with unfailing regularity, witnesses for God to the nations of the world, drawing renewed hope and strength to carry them through whatever suffering and persecution the rolling years may bring along. He that delivered His people from Pharaoh, Haman, the Hitlers and the Stalins, will not fail His people whatever betide.

Passover—the story of deliverance, the harbinger of a greater redemption yet to come, the vehicle of the undying Messianic hope.

The Last Passover in the Upper Room

During a recent visit to the Land of Israel I stood on the Mount of Zion overlooking the ancient city of Jerusalem, with Gethsemane, Calvary, and the Mount of Olives on the near horizon. Close by is an ancient house with one room called the "Coenaculum." This is the "Upper Room" where the Lord Jesus Christ and His twelve disciples ate their passover meal and where Jesus ordained the most sacred rite among Christians, the Lord's Supper, commemorating His death, resurrection, and coming again.

It was here in this Upper Room that Passover at last obtained its real meaning and deepest significance.

Let us turn in our minds to that great event where the Lord and His twelve disciples gathered together in this room to eat the passover. How His heart yearned to sit down with His nearest family, the twelve.

"Seven days shall ye eat unleavened bread"
—Exodus 12:15

Happy Yemenite woman carrying supply of unleavened bread for Passover

"With desire I have desired to eat this passover with you before I suffer"—Luke 22:15.

Here they sat together observing the passover as ordered by God in Exodus 12. But what new life was now infused into this ancient observance by the One who was the final reality of the passover story.

Now the full significance of Israel's deliverance from Egypt was at last unfolded. Here was "the Lamb of God" in the person of the Messiah Himself, about to shed His blood upon the cross, that all men who believe in Him may be set free from the Egypt of sin and darkness and enabled to begin a new life as children of God.

Among the many symbolic actions of the passover there is the eating of the "Aphikomen." Early in the meal the father takes the middle matzo of the three unleavened cakes, breaks it, and after pronouncing a benediction, distributes half among the members of the family, while the second half is hidden away and brought forth at the end of the meal.

Even so the Lord Jesus Christ sat down with His disciples and took the bread, blessed it, broke it, and divided it among His disciples, saying,

"Take, eat: this is my body, which is broken for you: this do in remembrance of me"—1 Corinthians 11:24.

How strange that the hidden half of the unleavened middle cake should be preserved as a symbol and rite even to the present day—a wonderful testimony to the broken body of the Lord Jesus Christ and His resurrection. Strange and beyond explanation are the wonderful ways of our God.

The red wine on the passover table brings to memory the blood of the lamb whereby the children of Israel were saved from death. Our Saviour too drank of that red wine after blessing it and dividing it among His disciples, saying,

"This cup is the new testament in my blood: this do ye, as oft as ye drink it, in remembrance of me"—1 Corinthians 11:25.

He Himself was the final reality of what the passover lamb sought to convey originally. It is His blood that saves Jew and Gentile alike from the death of sin and eternal condemnation and makes the believer a child of God.

The Hymn the Lord Sang

At the end of the passover celebration the Hallel or Psalms 113-118 are sung. In Psalm 118:21-24 we find the words:

I will praise thee: for thou has heard me, and art become my salvation.

The stone which the builders refused is become the head stone of the corner.

This is the Lord's doing; it is marvelous in our eyes.

This is the day which the Lord hath made; we will rejoice and be glad in it.

Those were even the very words which our Lord and His disciples sang after the passover feast. As we read:

"When they had sung an hymn, they went out into the Mount of Olives"—Matthew 26:30.

In the mouth of our Lord the words of the Psalm take on a remarkable significance. He Himself was the stone which the builders rejected and the corner stone of God's mighty edifice, His kingdom. Christ, the foundation and cornerstone, the Alpha and Omega, the sanctuary of God in whom men of all generations and every race have found refuge and peace for their souls. "This is the Lord's doing" and indeed "it is marvelous in our eyes."

And so the Passover and the Lord's supper merge into one complete story of deliverance and salvation. Every time a Jew partakes of the passover, unconsciously he bears witness to the Messiah. Every time a Christian partakes of the Lord's Supper he remembers Him of whom the passover lamb was a portrayal, the Messiah who died for him and by whose blood we are cleansed and forgiven.

Christ Arose — as David Foretold

The story of the Passover and the Lord's Supper would be incomplete without the resurrection of our Lord. The story of Jesus does not end with His death upon the cross and the burial in a borrowed grave. If this were the end the cross would signify a beautiful but tragic life. But Christ arose the victor over death, raised up by the power of God according to His Word, that He would not suffer His Holy One to see corruption—Psalm 16:10.

Christ arose, the first fruits of resurrection, bringing to all believers assurance that if we die in Him we shall also live through Him and with Him.

"But now is Christ risen from the dead, and become the first fruits of them that slept.

For since by man came death, by man came also the resurrection of the dead. For as in Adam all die, even so in Christ shall all be made alive"—1 Corinthians 15:20-22.

Today on Mount Zion there is a shrine dear

11

to the hearts of Jews throughout the world. It holds the tomb of David, beloved King of the Jews, upon which engraved with golden Hebrew letters are the words, "David the King of Israel lives for evermore."

I am sure the Apostle Peter must have known this tomb for he speaks about it quite clearly in the Acts of the Apostles, when on the Day of Pentecost he addressed a large number of Jews in Jerusalem, saying:

"Men and brethen, let me freely speak unto you of the partiarch David, that he is both dead and buried, and his sepulchre is with us unto this day.

Therefore being a prophet, and knowing that God had sworn with an oath to him, that of the fruit of his loins, according to the flesh, he would raise up Christ to sit on his throne;

Tomb of David on Mount Zion
"Men and brethren, let me freely speak unto you of the patriarch David, that he is both dead and buried, and his sepulchre is with us unto this day"—Acts 2:29

He seeing this before spake of the resurrection of Christ, that his soul was not left in hell, neither his flesh did see corruption.

This Jesus hath God raised up, whereof we all are witnesses"—Acts 2:29-32.

As a result of this sermon 3,000 souls surrendered in faith to the Messiah. The first church of Christ consisting of 3,000 believers was established in Jerusalem.

Christ our Passover

The Apostle Paul, writing by the Holy Spirit, summed up the significance of this Passover for every child of God, when he wrote:

"Christ our passover is sacrificed for us: Therefore let us keep the feast, not with old leaven, neither with the leaven of malice and wickedness; but with the unleavened bread of sincerity and truth"—1 Corinthians 5:7,8.

Contemplating the story of the Passover and the story of the crucifixion and resurrection of the Lord Jesus Christ, the words of the beloved disciple come to mind:

"Behold, what manner of love the Father hath bestowed upon us, that we should be called the sons of God"—1 John 3:1.

Chapter Two

The Feast of Weeks—
Pentecost

Rite and Reality

THREE times a year were the Israelites commanded to appear before God in the Holy Temple in Jerusalem. The occasions were the Passover, celebrating deliverance from Egypt and symbolized by the eating of the unleavened bread and the offering of the Passover lamb; Pentecost, or the Feast of Weeks, typified by the offering of two wave loaves made of newly harvested wheat; and the Feast of Tabernacles, symbolized by the booths, commemorating Israel's wandering through the wilderness and final entrance into the Land of Promise—Deuteronomy 16:16.

The word Pentecost is Greek, meaning fifty. It was so designated because it was observed on the fiftieth day after the Passover Sabbath. These are the words of the institution of Pentecost in the Old Testament:

"And ye shall count unto you from the **morrow after the Sabbath from the day that ye brought the sheaf of the wave-offering; seven sabbaths shall be complete:**

"Even unto the morrow after the seventh sabbath shall ye number fifty days; and ye shall offer a new meat-offering unto the Lord."

"Ye shall bring out of your habitations **two wave-loaves** of two tenth deals: They shall be of **fine flour;** They shall be **baken with leaven;**

14

they are the firstfruits unto the Lord"—
Leviticus 23:15-17.

In another place in the book of Exodus
(34:22) it is briefly described thus:

"And thou shalt observe the **feast of weeks,**
of the **firstfruits of wheat harvest,** and the
feast of ingathering at the year's end."

For centuries Israel was an agricultural
people depending for her sustenance on the
produce of the land. Pentecost was the Feast
of the Ingathering of the firstfruits of the
wheat harvest, a thanksgiving festival in
which Israel expressed her dependence on God
for harvest and daily bread.

The Feast of Weeks was a most popular
holiday, falling in early summer when the

*"The first of the firstfruits of thy land thou
shalt bring into the house of the Lord thy God"*
—Exodus 23:19

15

cloudless skies of the Promised Land are blue and benign, the weather caressingly warm, and generally unmarred by the scorching desert wind, the Hamsin.

From every part of the country Jews would stream to Jerusalem to appear before their God. Also visitors from abroad from among the diaspora of Israel, would gather for the Feast of Weeks.

In time, when the Jews became dispersed among the nations, Pentecost lost its primary character as a harvest festival, and became know as "The Feast of the Giving of the Law." Ancient Rabbis by careful calculation and time reckoning came to the conclusion that God gave the law to Moses on the Day of Pentecost. Hence Pentecost is also known as "The Season of the Giving of the Law," and is a time of rejoicing among the Jews.

Pentecost the Birthday of Judaism

Being the anniversary of the giving of the Law on Mount Sinai, Pentecost is considered as the birthday of Judaism.

In Leviticus 23:11 we read that on the morrow after the Sabbath, that is the Passover Sabbath, the priest was to bring the sheaf of the wave offering into the Temple, signifying the beginning of the new harvest, the beginning of the firstfruit.

How strangely these words were to become prophetic of the one who on the morrow after the Passover Sabbath was to rise from the dead and to become the "firstfruits of the Resurrection" (1 Corinthians 15:20).

Then on the Day of Pentecost "two wave-loaves" were brought to the Lord, loaves made

16

of fine flour ground of the new wheat and baked with leaven. Of all the cereal offerings, alone the wave-loaves were baked with leaven. Why leaven? And why **two** wave-loaves? Leaven is symbolic of sin. The Passover bread was unleavened because it signified the sinless body of Christ, who being without sin became sin for our sakes. But the two wave-loaves were symbolic of Israel in whom there is the leaven of sin.

Pentecost the Birthday of the Church

Fifteen hundred years had passed since God commanded His people through Moses to observe the Feast of Weeks. Much had happened in that time. Prophets came and went, all foretelling the coming of a Saviour to redeem Israel from sin. At last He who was prophesied, Jesus the Messiah, came. He was crucified according to the eternal purpose of God. He died to save Israel. Then He rose, according to prophecy, and before ascending to Heaven He commanded His disciples to wait in Jerusalem until they would be endued with the Holy Spirit. They waited forty-nine days after His resurrection, even as the Jews waited forty-nine days from Passover to Pentecost.

"And when the day of Pentecost was fully come, they were all with one accord in one place.

"And suddenly there came a sound from heaven as of a rushing mighty wind, and it filled all the house where they were sitting.

"And there were dwelling at Jerusalem Jews, devout men, out of every nation under heaven."—Acts 2:1,2,5.

On this Day of Pentecost, Peter addressed his countrymen from every part of the world, who came to Jerusalem, and also a number of Gentile proselytes, witnessing to them concerning Christ, and ending with this exhortation, "save yourselves from this untoward generation" (verse 40).

And such was the power of the Holy Spirit working in Peter that we read:

"They that gladly received his word were baptized: and the same day there were added unto them about three thousand souls.

"And they continued stedfastly in the apostles' doctrine and fellowhip, and in breaking of bread, and in prayers"—(Acts 2:41-42).

Thus the church of Christ, made up of 3000 Jews and some Gentile proselytes, was born.

Now we are beginning to see the meaning of the **two** wave-loaves baked with leaven. For the church of Christ of which both Jew and Gentile are members is not without sin. It contains leaven, the symbol of sin, reminding us to look for perfection **not** in the church, but in **Him,** the perfect Son of God, in whom there is no leaven of sin.

The 3000 Jewish believers were the spiritual firstfruits of the church of Christ. Thus the Old Testament symbol, the two wave-loaves, became a glorious reality in the New—A Church composed of Jewish and Gentile believers, purchased by the blood of the Lamb.

Ruth the Ancestress of Jesus

On the Day of Pentecost the Jews even until the present day read the book of Ruth. This they do for two reasons. Because the Book of Ruth has a rustic setting—Bethlehem at harvest time. Thus it is preeminently suitable for a harvest festival. Then also it presents Ruth the Moabitess, a Gentile woman, who came to know and to love the God of Naomi, the Jewess. Here hope and prophecy combine. They look to the day when Jew and Gentile shall worship God together through the kinsman Redeemer, Christ, typified by Boaz, the friend and husband of Ruth, his Gentile bride.

In Ruth we have a gracious story of love, faithfulness, and friendship stronger than death, a story unmatched and unsurpasssed in all the literature of the world.

Let us listen to the grief-sticken widow, Naomi, as she speaks to her Gentile daughters-

Ruth and Boaz

19

in-law, who lost their husbands, her sons, through famine.

"And Naomi said unto her two daughters-in-law, Go, return each to her mother's house: the Lord deal kindly with you, as ye have dealt with the dead, and with me.

"The Lord grant you that ye may find rest, each of you in the house of her husband. Then she kissed them; and they lifted up their voice, and wept" (Ruth 1:8,9).

Orpah let herself be persuaded to leave her mother-in-law, but Ruth clave to her. Then Naomi spake again:

"And she said, behold, thy sister-in-law is gone back unto her people, and unto her gods: return thou after thy sister-in-law.

"And Ruth said, intreat me not to leave thee, or to return from following after thee: for whither thou goest, I will go; and where thou lodgest, I will lodge: **thy people shall be my people, and thy God my God:**

"Where thou diest, will I die, and there will I be buried: the Lord do so to me, and more also, if ought but death part thee and me.

"When she saw that she was stedfastly minded to go with her, she left speaking unto her" (Ruth 1:15-18).

Lovely Ruth, the Gentile woman of Moab, came to be not only a child of the God of Abraham, Isaac, and Jacob, but an ancestress of King David, and his greater Son, Jesus the Messiah (Matthew 1:1-16).

The Spiritual Commonwealth of Israel

Pentecost of the old Jewish dispensation was pointing to the time when Jew and Gentile should come to know and worship the one Holy

God of Israel. In Christ alone this vision becomes a reality. Today saved Jews and Gentiles are united in one church, of which the Lord Jesus Christ is both the cornerstone and head.

The Apostle Paul writing to the Ephesians speaks of this Church of Christ as the spiritual commonwealth of Israel, describing it movingly in this way:

"Wherefore remember, that ye being in time past Gentiles in the flesh, who are called Uncircumcision by that which is called the Circumcision in the flesh made by hands;

"That at that time ye were without Christ, being aliens from the commonwealth of Israel, and strangers from the covenants of promise, having no hope, and without God in the world:

"But now in Christ Jesus ye who sometimes were far off are made nigh by the blood of Christ.

"Now therefore ye are no more strangers and foreigners, but fellow-citizens with the saints, and of the household of God;

"And are built upon the foundation of the apostles and prophets, Jesus Christ himself being the chief corner stone;

"In whom all the building fitly framed together groweth unto an holy temple in the Lord:

"In whom ye also are builded together for an habitation of God through the Spirit"—Ephesians 2:11-13, 19-22.

The Mute Shall Speak Again

On the Day of Pentecost the Apostles being filled with the Holy Spirit spake in a multitude of tongues, witnessing for the Lord. Even today the Apostles of the Lord Jesus Christ, filled with His Spirit and love, go out to every nation and tongue and bring the Gospel of salvation in over 1000 tongues and dialects, not counting the cost, holding everything they have as dung for the sake of Christ their Saviour.

But Israel is still the mute servant of the Lord. Endowed with the gift of tongues as no other people, they still are mute as far as the carrying of the Gospel to the nations of the world is concerned.

It is significant and enlightening that those Children of Israel who have accepted the Lord Jesus Christ as their Messiah and Saviour have gone out to the nations with the Word of life and light. Their number is legion, for God has not left Himself without a witness among His people Israel, even from the first Jewish Apostles of the Messiah Jesus to our present generation. When He comes to make up His jewels, their names shall shine bright as the stars.

Oh, that the day may come when the Lord shall loosen the tongue of His servant Israel and they will go out to witness for Him in every part and corner of the earth, all their talents and gifts quickened and energized by the working of the Spirit of God in them.

Chapter Three

Rosh Hashana—New Year

ACTUALLY there are two New Years in Judaism. One, according to Biblical time reckoning begins on the first day of the month of Nisan or Abib, which means Spring. This month is roughly equivalent to our April. "And the Lord spake unto Moses and Aaron in the land of Egypt, saying, this month shall be unto you the beginning of months: it shall be the first month of the year to you"—Exodus 12:1,2.

The other, New Year's Day, which the Jews officially recognize and celebrate, is the first

Blowing of the Ram's Horn

day of the seventh month according to the Jewish calendar, and is called the month of Tishri.

In Leviticus 23:24 we read—"In the seventh month, in the first day of the month, shall ye have a **Sabbath, a memorial of blowing of trumpets, an holy convocation**".

The ancient Rabbis believed that the Lord created the world in the first week of the month of Tishri. Therefore the first day of the seventh month is considered the beginning of creation and the beginning of the year, and hence the present Jewish time reckoning. As it is generally known, the Jewish year is a lunar year which is shorter than the solar year by ten days and 21 hours. The year is divided into twelve lunar months of 28 or 29 days each. To equalize the difference betweeen the lunar and solar year, about every three years an extra month is added after the twelfth month, or March. This thirteen month year is the Jewish leap year.

The Sabbatical Month

Tishri being the seventh month of the year is a Sabbatical month. What the seventh day is to the week, Tishri, the seventh month, is to the year. Hence the first day is celebrated as a Sabbath, a day of rest and a memorial of blowing of trumpets, with a holy convocation.

In the book of Nehemiah (8:1-12) we read that after Israel came back from Bablylon they began again to observe the New Year Day solemnly. And when the law was read to them after long neglect, they were so overwhelmed that they broke down and cried and repented, until Ezra, their leader, had to comfort them and remind them that it was also a day of rejoicing and thanksgiving to the Lord, and that they were to go home comforted and to eat.

The Blowing of the Ram's Horn and its Significance

According to the Rabbis the blowing of the horns and trumpets ordained by the Lord and observed in the Temple in Jerusalem and throughout the Land of Israel, had a threefold purpose.

First, the trumpet sound called to repentance. It was as a call to the dead to arise and live again, to wake up from sin to regeneration through repentance.

Second, it had as its purpose to remind the Lord that He was in covenant relationship with His people Israel and to deal gently with them, not according to their merits but according to His gracious promises specially made to Abraham and to the patriarchs of old.

Third, it was to confound and to confuse Satan, who, the Rabbis thought, had a special predilection of accusing Israel on New Year's Day, bringing up before the Lord all their shortcomings and sins.

The horn used on the solemn occasion of the New Year's Day was a ram's horn, in order to bring to memory Abraham's sacrifice of his son Isaac at the Lord's command. This sacrifice was considered as if accomplished because of the absolute faith and willingness on the part of Abraham to do the Lord's bidding, but which God in His mercy refrained from exacting, substituting in the place of Isaac, a ram.

The Sacrifice of Isaac and the Sacrifice of the Son of God

The Jews make very much of Abraham's sacrifice of his son Isaac, referring to it again and again in their prayers, reminding God of Abraham and his faith which was willing to sacrifice Isaac. Abraham's sacrifice of Isaac typified gloriously the sacrifice of our Heavenly Father of His Son, the Lord Jesus Christ, and the willingness of the Son to offer Himself up for the salvation of all men. Isaac is a beautiful type of Christ.

In Genesis 22:6 we read: "And they went both of them together." Jesus said, "I and my Father are one". "I do always those things that please Him."

Divine Bookkeeping

New Year's Day is a solemn time of repentance and preparation for the Day of Atonement which follows ten days after. The Rabbis believe that during New Year, which lasts two days, the Lord opens three books. In one book the righteous are registered; in the second, are those who are neither wholly righteous nor utterly wicked; and in the third, the wicked are recorded.

The righteous are judged on New Year's Day and receive rewards such as life, welfare, prosperity, security from all manner of evil and harm, and peace.

In the Prayerbook of the Synagogue for the day of New Year we read the following prayer:

"In the book of life, blessing, peace and good sustenance may we be remembered and inscribed before thee, we and all thy people, the house of Israel, for a happy life and peace. Blessed art thou, O Lord, who makest peace."

The Ten Days of Repentance

The second book records the deeds good and bad of the intermediate group, those who are not wholly sinful nor altogether righteous. They are given ten days of repentance which are called Yomim Noraim, which means the fearsome or awesome days. During that period, depending on the sincerity of their repentance, the Lord will judge them on the Day of Atonement either for life or destruction, riches or poverty, health or hurt.

The wicked and unrepentant can expect only condemnation and death. Since, according to popular Jewish belief, the majority of mankind are neither utterly good nor utterly

Prayer in a Tel Aviv Synagogue

27

wicked, the ten days are of the utmost importance. Much therefore depends on the behavior and repentance of the Jew during these "Ten Awesome Days". During that period old enemies seek to make up their differences, charity is given to the poor, and long confessions of sins are repeated in the Synagogue prayers.

A New Year's Litany

The following is a typical although incomplete litany which Jews recite in Hebrew in the Synagogue on New Year's Day.

"Our Father, our King, we have sinned before thee.

Our Father, our King, we have no king beside thee.

Our Father, our King, renew unto us a happy year.

Our Father, our King, annul every severe decree concerning us.

Our Father, our King, annul the designs of those who hate us.

Our Father, our King, frustrate the counsel of our enemies.

Our Father, our King, stay the mouths of our adversaries and of those who accuse us.

Our Father, our King, remove pestilence, sword, famine, captivity and destruction from the children of thy covenant.

Our Father, our King, hold back the plague from thine heritage.

Our Father, our King, forgive and pardon all our iniquities.

Our Father, our King, blot out, and cause our transgressions and sins to pass away before thine eyes.

Our Father, our king, efface in thine abundant mercy all records of our guilt.

Our Father, our King, cause us to return unto thee in perfect repentance.

Our Father, our King, send perfect healing to the sick of thy people.

Our Father, our King, repeal the evil sentence of our judgment.

Our Father, our King, remember us in the book of happy life.

Our Father, our King, inscribe us in the book of redemption and salvation.

Our Father, our King, inscribe us in the book of sustenance and maintenance.

Our Father, our King, inscribe us in the book of merit.

Our Father, our King, inscribe us in the book of forgiveness and pardon.

Our Father, our King, cause salvation to spring forth for us.

Our Father, our King, exalt the horn of Israel thy people.

Our Father, our King, exalt the horn of thy Messiah."

The Glory Which Departed

In ancient days when the Temple existed there were special sacrifices offered consisting of two young bullocks, one ram and seven lambs of the first year without spot (Numbers 28:11-15). At the offering of these sacrifices over a hundred priests officiated and the trumpets and shophar were blown.

But these sacrifices like all the Temple details were merely a forecast of the perfect sacrifice fulfilled in the person of the Lord

29

Jesus Christ. We who have been washed and redeemed by His blood are eternally grateful that we have been bought with a great price. Although "It is not possible that the blood of bulls and of goats should take away sins," His blood avails for evermore.

New Year's Call to Repentance

Prophetically New Year marks a further stage in God's plan of salvation for Israel first, but then also for all mankind. Passover was the beginning of redemption wrought through the blood of the Lamb, foreshadowing the Lord Jesus Christ, "the Lamb of God which taketh away the sin of the world."

Pentecost, the Feast of First Fruits, is the birthday of Judaism and signifies also the birth of the Church of Christ. This is followed by a long period between the solemn Holy Days of Pentecost and New Year's Day, typifying Israel's long period of estrangement from God and life in exile.

Then comes the Feast of New Year presenting a call to repentance and an opportunity to be reconciled with God, on the Day of Atonement which follows ten days after New Year's Day. Then comes the Feast of Tabernacles and Harvest, symbolic of the completion of the Church of God through the final ingathering of those who are to be saved, Jew and Gentile alike, into the Body of Christ.

The Apostle Paul was well acquainted with all the Jewish feasts, with all the rites, hopes, and prophetic implications inherent in them. Was he thinking of Rosh Hashana and the blowing of rams' horns, the bugle call to repentance, when he cried out: "Wherefore he saith, Awake thou that sleepest, and arise from the dead, and Christ shall give thee light!"—Ephesians 5:14.

Chapter Four

Yom Kippur—
Day of Atonement

YOM Kippur or the Day of Atonement begins at sundown at the end of the ninth day of Tishri, the seventh month of the Bible year. Of all Jewish holy occasions this is the most solemn—"The Sabbath of Sabbaths." The elaborate ritual for the Day of Atonement as observed in the Tabernacle and the Temple is described in Leviticus 16.

Yom Kippur is a solemn fast day. For twenty-four awesome hours from sundown to sunset, Jews the world over, young and old, male and female, assemble in synagogues and places of prayer, to seek atonement with God and forgiveness for all their sins. It is "The Day" of judgment and reckoning.

Between New Year's Day and Yom Kippur are ten days which are called "THE TEN DAYS OF REPENTANCE", or "THE AWESOME DAYS". Every Jew during that period searches his heart and seeks to be reconciled with God and his neighbor.

Five days after Yom Kippur comes Succoth or The Feast of Tabernacles, lasting eight days. Then the whole cycle of the autumn holidays is concluded with "Simchath Torah"— The Rejoicing over the Law.

Preparation for Day of Atonement

New Year's Day on the first of Tishri opens the solemn period of repentance preparatory for Yom Kippur. In the afternoon of New Year's Day, Jews throughout the world assemble near rivers, brooks, and oceans to cast away their sins. This ceremony is called TASHLIKH and is based on Micah 7:19.

"He will turn again, he will have compassion upon us; he will subdue our iniquities; and THOU WILT CAST ALL THEIR SINS (in Hebrew—Tashlikh) INTO THE DEPTHS OF THE SEA."

Wherever Jews honor the traditions of Israel, "Tashlikh" is observed. In the afternoon of New Year's Day you may see crowds of Jews near larger bodies of water performing the symbolic ritual of "CASTING AWAY THEIR SINS".

Substitutes for the Atoning Sacrifice

Since the Jews have no temple, priest or sacrifice, substitutes for the atoning sacrifice have been provided by the rabbis. Some of these are repentance, which includes reparation of wrong, prayer, and fasting. Of all substitutes, REPENTANCE, PRAYER, AND CHARITY, are considered the most important. Also a rooster for every male, and a hen for a female, are used as substitutes for the atoning sacrifice. These sacrifices of hens and roosters are called KAPPOROTH, which means propitiatory or atoning sacrifices. Needless to say these Kapporoth or sacrifices of roosters and hens have no basis in the Word of God, but are rather the expression of a deep sense of need for atonement through the shedding of blood.

Another substitute for sacrifice is CHARITY. It is significant that the word "charity" in modern Hebrew usage is the same as "righteousness".

One's own SUFFERINGS are also considered a substitute, especially the sufferings of the righteous. (Note the striking similarity of this and other rabbinical traditions to Roman Catholicism).

Among the orthodox Jews of Eastern Europe there use to be the custom to inflict upon themselves 39 stripes called "MALKOTH". We recall that the Apostle Paul was on five occasions subjected to "forty stripes save one"—an ancient Jewish method of corporal punishment for transgressors.

Another substitute for the sacrifice of Atonement, according to the rabbis is one's own DEATH. The rabbis base this mistaken idea on Psalm 116:15, "Precious in the sight of the Lord is the death of His saints."

THE STUDY OF THE LAW, especially of the Talmud, is another one of the substitutes.

A whole month before the Day of Atonement, special prayers are offered at midnight for forgiveness. These prayers are known as SLIHOTH—prayers for forgiveness.

In the afternoon preceding the Day of Atonement, a festive meal is consumed by the family in preparation for the ensuing fast. On the Day of Atonement a complete fast is observed, which excludes even the moistening of one's parched lips with water. THIS FAST is incumbent upon every Israelite from the age of 13 upward. Dispensations are granted only to those dangerously ill.

The Day of Atonement services begin at sundown when the cantor, surrounded by two members of the congregation and dressed in a white garb and headgear, addresses himself to the assembly in the Synagogue with this solemn preamble:

"By authority of the Court on high, and by authority of the Court on earth, with the knowledge of the All-Present and with the knowledge of this congregation, we give leave to pray with them that have transgressed."

Kol Nidrei—All Vows

After that the cantor begins in a chanting voice the most solemn prayer of the Yom Kippur devotions. This is known as Kol Nidrei —"All Vows". In somber solemn chanting tones he recites:

"All vows, bonds, oaths, devotions, promises, penalties, and obligations: wherewith we have vowed, sworn, devoted and bound ourselves: from this Day of Atonement unto the next Day of Atonement, may it come unto us for good: lo, all these, we repent us in them. They shall be absolved, released, annulled, made void, and of none effect: They shall not be binding nor shall they have any power. Our vows shall not be vows; our bonds shall not be bonds: and our oaths shall not be oaths."

This prayer which the Jews consider as one of the most sacred has often been criticized as a prayer that absolves all Jews from any form of promise and obligation. But in fact the prayer of Kol-Nidrei merely expresses a deep consciousness of the inability of man to keep in full his vows, promises, bonds and obligations in relation to God, and is always, no matter how conscientious, on the debit side of the ledger. Man can only face his Maker as a suppliant in need of forgiveness.

The Meaning of Yom Kippur

The word Yom Kippur itself meaning the Day of Atonement, comes from a Hebrew word Kapper, "to cover". According to this meaning, God covers the sins of His people by the blood of the sacrifice. Thus seeing only the penalty paid and the person covered with the blood, he appears sinless before Him. This expresses perfectly the idea of substitutionary death and propitiation. It points to the heart of the Gospel: "Christ died for our sins"— I Corinthians 15:3.

Another interpretation of the root of the word Kapper is "Kofer", which means a ransom, as in Exodus 21:30.

"If there be laid on him a sum of money, then he shall give for the ransom of his life whatsoever is laid upon him."

Or in II Samuel 21:3 when the blood of the murdered Gibeonites cried to heaven for vengeance, David said, "Wherewith shall I make the atonement," and the word there is Kapper. The underlying idea is that there is no atonement except through the blood of the sacrifice. On this all the Jewish commentators are very clear. The Talmud says, Yoma 5a, "There is no atonement except with blood." And in the New Testament, we read in Hebrews 9:22, "Without the shedding of blood is no remission."

The Day of Atonement Sacrifices

To the appointed sacrifice of the Day of Atonement according to Scripture (Leviticus 16), belong two goats. One of these was the scapegoat, in Hebrew "Azazel", which carried away all the sins of the Children of Israel into an uninhabited place. "Azazel" therefore was a type of Christ who was led forth without the city walls, bearing the sins of His people (Leviticus 16:21, 22; Matthew 27:33).

The second goat was killed by the High Priest in the Temple and its blood sprinkled to make atonement for all the uncleanness and transgressions of the Children of Israel.

In addition to the goats there were also the sacrifices of lambs and bullocks. An important part in the Day of Atonement ritual was played by the red heifer which was killed and its blood sprinkled for the cleansing of the people from all defilement of sin (Numbers 19; Hebrews 9:13).

The High Priest as Mediator

The High Priest assisted by over 500 priests performed the most solemn and elaborate rites of Yom Kippur. He was separated for seven days from the people, preparing for the solemn day. On the Day of Atonement the High Priest washed his body five times and ten times his hands and his feet.

The climax of the Day of Atonement was when the High Priest entered the Most Holy Place where the Ark of the Covenant was placed and the "Mercy Seat" overshadowed it. Above it was the Shekinah Glory—the visible presence of God in a cloud.

After killing the bullock and the second goat set apart for Jehovah, he sprinkled the Most Holy Place and the veil, the altar of incense and the altar of burnt-offering, cleansing them from the defilement of sin. He then appeared before the very presence of God, imploring the Lord by His mysterious and sacred Name "Jehovah".

The Sacred Tetragrammaton

Only the officiating priests were initiated in the secret of the proper pronunciation of the sacred Tetragrammaton YHWH, the holy, mystical, and ineffable name of JEHOVAH. The common people simply dreaded to use the name of God for it was instilled into their very fibre, "Thou shalt not take the name of the Lord thy God in vain." Even today, orthodox Jews are loath to use the word "Jehovah" in any manner.

It is interesting to know among the many things of which the Jews accused our Saviour, according to the ancient tradition of rabbis, was the alleged fact that the Lord Jesus somehow misappropriated the sacred pronunciation of the name of Jehovah from the High Priest, and thereby performed miracles. It seems this was an effort on the part of the rabbis to account for the peculiar relationship between our Lord Jesus and His Heavenly Father, and His position as Mediator between man and God.

While the High Priest was in the Most Holy Place in the very presence of God, the people meantime with mounting tension waited for the reappearance of the High Priest, in dreadful fear lest his prolonged absence in the Holy of Holies signify that God had not forgiven His people and had slain their unworthy High Priest.

When at last the High Priest came out of the Most Holy Place, the people sighed with relief that their service was accepted, their sins forgiven.

Shadow and Reality

A careful study of the Epistle to the Hebrews gives the New Testament believer a deeper understanding of the Temple service and its sacrifices, the position of the High Priest, and the symbolism of all the rites in their relation to Christ. Without the New Testament, the Old Testament is incomplete, a promise without fulfillment, a shadow without reality. Here we have a divine commentary on the Temple, the High Priest and the sacrifices—all pointing to and speaking of Christ.

"But Christ being come an high priest of good things to come, by a greater and more perfect tabernacle, not made with hands, that is to say, not of this building;

Neither by the blood of goats and calves, but by his own blood he entered in once into the holy place, having obtained eternal redemption for us.

For if the blood of bulls and of goats, and the ashes of an heifer sprinkling the unclean, sanctifieth to the purifying of the flesh;

How much more shall the blood of Christ, who through the eternal Spirit offered himself without spot to God, purge your conscience from dead works to serve the living God?

For when Moses had spoken every precept to all the people according to the law, he took the blood of calves and of goats, with water, and scarlet wool, and hyssop, and sprinkled both the book, and all the people,

Saying, This is the blood of the testament which God hath enjoined unto you.

Moreover he sprinkled with blood both the tabernacle, and all the vessels of the ministry.

And almost all things are by the law purged with blood; and without the shedding of blood is no remission"—Hebrews 9:11-14, 19-22.

It is this Christ who is our atonement and perfect mediator with God. In Him all the verities of the Old Testament, the Temple, the High Priest, the sacrifices, have been embodied and fulfilled.

"So Christ was once offered to bear the sins of many; and unto them that look for him shall he appear the second time without sin unto salvation"—Hebrews 9:28.

"The Mighty Holiness of this Day"

Deprived of Temple, priest and sacrifice, Rabbinical Judaism has made a consistent effort to water down the importance of the sacrifices and the shed blood which alone makes atonement for the soul. In place of the atonements, the Day of Atonement itself has been declared to make atonement for sinners, without the necessity of a sacrifice. This view is reflected in the prayer of Rabbi Amnon of Mayence (circa 1100 A.D.). Rabbi Amnon of Mayence is believed to have been a martyr for his Jewish faith. The Archbishop of Mayence urged the Rabbi to renounce Judaism and to be baptized. The Rabbi steadfastly refused. The exasperated Archbishop ordered that the Rabbi's hands and feet be mutilated. Dying from his wounds, Rabbi Amnon is said to have composed this prayer in the synagogue on the eve of Yom Kippur.

"We will celebrate the mighty holiness of this day, for it is one of awe and terror. Thereon is thy dominion exalted and thy throne is established in mercy, and thou sittest thereon in truth. Verily it is thou alone who art judge and arbiter, who knowest and art witness; thou writest down and settest the

40

seal, thou recordest and tellest; yea, thou rememberest the things forgotten. Thou unfoldest the records, and the deeds therin inscribed proclaim themselves; for lo! the seal of every man's hand is set thereto.

"The great trumpet is sounded; the still small voice is heard; the angels are dismayed; fear and trembling seize hold of them as they proclaim, Behold the Day of Judgment! The host of heaven is to be arraigned in judgment. For in thine eyes they are not pure; and all who enter the world dost thou cause to pass before thee as a flock of sheep. As a shepherd seeketh out his flock, and causeth them to pass beneath his crook, so dost thou cause to pass and number, tell and visit every living soul, appointing the measure of every creature's life and decreeing their destiny."

The underlying belief of this prayer is that atonement and forgiveness depend on whether a man's good deeds and merits outweigh his misdeeds and demerits. The basic weakness of Judaism is that it is aware of "sins" but ignores "sin"—the essential bias of man toward evil, the sinfulness of man's very nature.

Inscribed and Sealed

On Yom Kippur God seals the books of accounting which have been opened on New Year's Day. Whereas before New Year's Day, Jews wish one another that their name be "inscribed" into the book of life, after New Year's Day and before the Day of Atonement, when greeting one another or sending greetings in writing, the word is "may you be 'sealed' in the book of life."

To the child of God who knows the holiness,

41

the righteousness and the purity of God, to have to depend on one's merits or demerits is rather a bleak prospect. King David, one of the most lovely personalities in the Old Testament, conscious deeply of his own sin, cried out:

"If thou, Lord, shouldest mark iniquities, O Lord, who shall stand?"—Psalm 130:3.

Messianic Echoes of Yom Kippur

In spite of Yom Kippur, the day dedicated to atonement, there is no assurance of sins forgiven in Judaism. There is longing, there is hope for forgiveness, but of assurance, there is none. This only the Son of God can give to those who come to Him in faith. The Day of Atonement is only a substitute for Atonement. Judaism could be best summed up as man's attempt to justify himself by his own effort, without the atonement made by a Saviour. That cannot be done. There can be no substitute for Christ, our Atonement and Propitiator. Judaism has tried hard to find a substitute for Him. Unscriptural, so-called Christianity, is trying hard even today. The result is only a man-made substitute religion, which increases the abyss between God and man.

Deep in her heart Israel knows that her atonement is of the Messiah. He alone is able to bring forgiveness. To this gives witness an ancient prayer in the Day of Atonement liturgy which refers plainly to Isaiah 53 in the following plaintive and wistful lines;

"Our righteous Messiah has departed from us,

We are horror-stricken, and have none to justify us.

42

*Our iniquities and the yoke of our
 transgressions
He carries who is wounded because of our
 transgressions.
He bears on His shoulder the burden of
 our sins,
To find pardon for all our iniquities.
By His stripes we shall be healed—
O Eternal one, it is time that thou
 shouldest create Him anew!"*

Here we see clearly that Judaism is without true atonement, and there is only a wistful yearning for the same. It looks to the Messiah to bring salvation and reconciliation with God.

The Shofar—The Trump of God

And so the Yom Kippur solemnities are completed by blowing of the Shofar, the ram's horn, the trumpet which heralds the coming of the Messiah. Here the Hope of Israel and the Hope of the Christian converge. Israel waits for His first coming, while the believer in the Lord Jesus Christ knows that He already came and saved him. He now looks forward to His Second Coming when He shall establish His Kingdom on the earth.

"For the Lord Himself shall descend from heaven with a shout, with the voice of the archangel, and with the trump of God: and the dead in Christ shall rise first:

Then we which are alive and remain shall be caught up together with them in the clouds, to meet the Lord in the air: and so shall we ever be with the Lord"—I Thessalonians 4:16, 17.

One day the Hope of Israel and the Hope of the Church will at last become a reality. The King of Glory shall come. But the face of the

King will be one—that of the Lord Jesus Christ, the Messiah of Israel, the hope of all nations.

Chapter Five

Succoth—The Feast of Tabernacles or Booths

"Also in the fifteenth day of the seventh month, when ye have gathered in the fruit of the land, ye shall keep a feast unto the Lord seven days: on the first day shall be a sabbath, and on the eighth day shall be a sabbath.

"And ye shall take you on the first day the boughs of goodly trees, branches of palm trees, and the boughs of thick trees, and willows of the brook; and ye shall rejoice before the Lord your God seven days.

"And ye shall keep it a feast unto the Lord seven days in the year. It shall be a statue for ever in your generations: ye shall celebrate it in the seventh month.

"Ye shall dwell in booths seven days; all that are Israelites born shall dwell in booths:

"That your generations may know that I made the children of Israel to dwell in booths, when I brought them out of the land of Egypt: I am the Lord your God"—Leviticus 23:39-43.

An Agricultural and Thanksgiving Festival

THE Feast of Tabernacles comes on the 15th of Tishri, the seventh month according to the Bible calendar. This usually coincides with the end of September or early October.

Jews the world over, from Bombay to Brooklyn, and from Jerusalem to San Francisco, are busy erecting booths, according to the prescription the Lord gave to them through Moses in Leviticus 23:33-44.

The Feast of Tabernacles is one of the three great occasions upon which God commanded the Children of Israel to assemble in the Temple of Jerusalem, and present their sacrifices and offerings unto the Lord. "They shall not appear before the Lord empty"— Deuteronomy 16:16.

The Feast is primarily agricultural in its character. It is a joyous occasion. The harvest has been brought in from the fields, the groves and the orchards. Barns and sheds are full. Hearts, too, are full of praise and thanksgiving for God's bounties. It is "The Feast of Ingathering," or Israel's Thanksgiving Festival—"The Feast," as the Gospel of John 7:37 calls it.

The Rabbis say, "He who has not seen Jerusalem during the Feast of Tabernacles does not know what rejoicing means." With a little imagination one can see God's people streaming toward the Holy Temple, from every town, village and hamlet in Israel, and from distant lands abroad. They bring their tithes and freewill offerings, and fulfilled vows. At that time the emptied Temple treasury was opened, to be filled again by the gifts of the faithful, so that the poor and the needy throughout the land might be satisfied.

The Feast of Tabernacles—Commemorative

Apart from its agricultural character, the Feast of Tabernacles also commemorates God's mighty deliverance of His people from Egypt and their 40 years of wilderness wandering, when they dwelt in tents and tabernacles.

Israel must never forget that for 40 years they were led by the hand of God, nor that they were pilgrims to a better land where God abideth.

And so for the last 3500 years Jews have been observing Succoth, the Feast of Booths, building little tabernacles or booths, with walls of plaited branches and with thatched roofs, which afford shade by day, but permit the stars to gaze down by night upon the Children of Israel as they faithfully fulfill the ancient command: "Ye shall dwell in booths seven days."

The Lulav and the Ethrog

In ancient times there was a controversy between the Sadducees and the Pharisees concerning the booths. The Sadducees held that the "boughs of goodly trees" pertained to the building of the booths. The Pharisees on the other hand were of the opinion that the branches were meant to be carried in the hands by the celebrating people. This they called the lulav. Eventually a compromise was reached. The booths of branches satisfied the Sadducees. In addition the people used in their celebration a lulav which is made of branches of palms, myrtles and willows, all fastened with a golden thread. These branches of palms or "lulav" were waved in the Temple during certain parts of the service.

Beside the lulav, every Jew came to the Temple holding an "ethrog," or citrus fruit, symbolic of the fruit of the Promised Land. The booths, the lulav, and the ethrog, or citrus fruit, are basic symbols of the Feast of Tabernacles.

My, what a beautiful lulav!

The Prophetic Character of the Feast of Tabernacles

Numerous sacrifices were offered in the Temple—bullocks, rams and goats—for a sin-offering. The first day of the Feast thirteen bullocks were offered, twelve the next day, eleven the third, diminishing every day until seven bullocks were offered on the seventh day, making a total of seventy.

The Rabbis explain that this number of seventy bullocks was a sacrifice on behalf of the seventy nations of the world, looking toward their conversion to the God of Israel and their gathering under the Shekinah glory.

The Feast of Tabernacles, like the other feasts of Israel, focuses the attention of God's people both on the past, on what God has done, and on the future, on what God will do. The prophetic message of the Feast of Tabernacles is that there is shelter in the Tabernacle of God under the wings of the Shekinah glory, for the Jew first, and also the Gentile nations.

Wells of Salvation

There were two outstanding features which characterized the Temple service of the Feast of Tabernacles. (1) The pouring of water in the Temple. (2) The brilliant illumination of the Temple.

A specially appointed priest was sent to the Pool of Siloam with a golden pitcher to bring water from the Pool. This was poured by the high priest into a basin at the foot of the altar. From another pitcher wine was poured into the same basin. These mingled together and flowed through special pipes back to the Brook of Kidron again.

The significance of the pouring of water was twofold. First, it was a symbolic and ritual prayer for abundant rain. Summer was at an end. Winter and the rainy season was about to begin. Upon abundant rain Israel then depended as now for her daily bread. Hence the prayers for the gates of Heaven to open and for abundant rain. Even today in the synagogue much prayer for rain is offered at this time. The pouring of water was a visual interpretation of God's grace in sending rain.

Secondly, the ritual of water libation went beyond the merely physical; it was prophetic and Messianic in its hope, looking toward the outpouring of the Holy Spirit not only upon Israel, but also the believers of all the nations under the reign of Messiah King.

The Day of the Great Hosanna

The ritual of water pouring lasted six days, climaxing on the seventh day, which concluded the Feast of Tabernacles. This day was called Hoshana Rabba, The Day of the Great Hosanna. It has a special messianic significance. The pouring of the water from the golden pitcher took place amidst the blasting of the trumpets by the priests and the singing of sacred music by the Levites, while the people, waving their lulavs, or palm branches, chanted the Hallel, Psalms 113-118.

The closing words of Psalm 118 are these:

"Save now, I beseech thee, O Lord: O Lord, I beseech thee, send now prosperity.

Blessed be he that cometh in the name of the Lord: we have blessed you out of the house of the Lord.

God is the Lord, which hath shewed us light: bind the sacrifice with cords, even unto the horns of the altar.

Thou art my God, and I will praise thee: thou art my God, I will exalt thee."

From the words "Save Now" (in Hebrew

"Hoshana"), this day was known as the "Great Hosanna." It was peculiarly Messianic in nature, a prayer for the speedy salvation through the Messiah. This is why our Saviour was greeted on another occasion with the waving of palm branches and the words, "Hosanna to the son of David,"meaning, "Save us Son of David." This is important for the understanding of what happened when the Lord attended the Temple service on the day of the "Great Hosanna."

It was while all this was going on, the pouring of the water from the Pool of Siloam into the altar basin, the blasting of the trumpets by the priests, the singing of the Psalms by the Levites, and the prayers of the people, "Save now, I beseech thee, O Lord," when the Messianic fervor was at the highest pitch, that the Lord Jesus stood in the Temple crying:

"If any man thirst, let him come unto me, and drink. He that believeth on me, as the scripture hath said, out of his belly shall flow rivers of living water"—John 7:38. What our Saviour said by implication was: "I am the answer to your prayers."

The Messianic claim of our Saviour was clearly understood by all. It must have come like a bolt from the blue. Here was the One claiming to be the answer to the fervent hope and prayer of long centuries and many generations. Could He, the carpenter's son of Nazareth, be the long expected Messiah?

"So there was a division among the People"—John 7:43.

In modern times the Jews observe on the last day of the Feast of Tabernacles, the Day of the Great Hosanna, the custom of striking

"The Arba'ah," the branches of the willow, three times in an effort to shed all the leaves, which represent sins.

A Messianic Prayer

At this time special Messianic prayers are said. Here is one of the prayers for the day:

A voice heralds, heralds and saith:

Turn unto me and be ye saved, today if ye hear my voice

Behold the man who sprang forth—Branch is his name—David himself

Stand up! Be buried in the dust no longer! Ye who dwell in the dust

Wake up and sing.

Glad will be the people when he ruleth

The name of the ungodly shall perish

But to His anointed, the Messiah David, he giveth grace

Grant salvation to the eternal people

To David and to his seed forever

The voice heralds and saith.

Upon the completion of this prayer the leaves of the willow branches are struck three times on the benches of the synagogue. With each falling leaf a sin falls away from the one who prays. But "The Man who sprang forth, the Messiah David," who alone is able to bring forgiveness of sins, is still unknown in Israel.

Temple Lights and the Light of the World

Another central feature of the Feast of Tabernacles was the illumination of the Temple in Jerusalem. The festive pilgrims came to the Temple bearing lights and torches, while in the Temple itself the golden candlesticks were lighted, transforming the Temple into one brilliant focus of light which illuminated most of Jerusalem and surroundings. What an eloquent symbol of the Sanctuary of God which was to be a light of the world!

Amidst all this splendor and the brilliant lights of the Temple, our Saviour stood proclaiming: "I am the light of the world."

Without true knowledge of the rites and symbols of the Feast of Tabernacles, we miss the profound significance of our Lord's pronouncements in the Temple.

Thus **the three aspects of the Feast of**

At Prayer in Jerusalem

Tabernacles stand out boldly: A harvest Thanksgiving, a national commemoration of redemption, and faith's leap into the future, when Jehovah shall gather the nations in the Messianic Kingdom of His blessed Son, the Lord Jesus.

With this in mind we understand the vision of Zechariah:

"And it shall come to pass, that every one that is left of all nations which came against Jerusalem shall even go up from year to year to worship the King, the Lord of hosts, and to keep the feast of tabernacles.

"And it shall be, that whoso will not come up of all the families of the earth unto Jerusalem to worship the King, the Lord of hosts, even upon them shall be no rain"— 14:16, 17.

Now we can understand why the punishment for the non-attendance at the Feast of Tabernacles was to be the withholding of the rain. The Feast of Tabernacles was preeminently the season when God vouchsafed to His people abundant rain. But beyond that, we see even further that the punishment for wilful refusal to come and worship the Lord must be the withholding of the outpouring of the blessed Holy Spirit from those who were invited to come but would not.

The Apostle John looking toward the greater Feast of Ingathering writes:

"After this I beheld, and, lo, a great multitude, which no man could number, of all nations, and kindreds, and people, and tongues, stood before the throne, and before the Lamb, clothed with white robes, and palms in their hands:

"And cried with a loud voice, saying, salvation (Hosanna) to our God which sitteth upon the throne, and unto the Lamb"— Revelation 7:9, 10.

Chapter Six

Simchath Torah—

(The Rejoicing over the Law)

THE Feast of Tabernacles is followed by Simchath Torah, which means literally "Rejoicing over the Law."

It arose in the early centuries when the system of reading the Law of Moses in the synagogues during the period of one year was established. On the Day of Rejoicing over the Law, the reading of the Book of Deuteronomy was completed and Genesis begun.

At this time all assembled in the synagogues are called upon to pronounce a blessing over the reading of the Law, and even boys partake. Little children come to the synagogues bearing colorful paper flags with gay inscriptions, extolling the Word of God.

The little flags have lighted candles burning on the flag rod, thrilling little boys and girls. In the synagogue the scrolls of the law, dressed in beautiful velvet mantles of red, scarlet, blue and white, and ornate with golden embroidery and inscriptions, are taken out from the ark of the Law, and placed lovingly in the arms of men and even little boys.

These scrolls, "The lively oracles of God," are the most precious possession of Israel. Men lived and died to preserve these for the generations yet unborn. Seven times they

"This is the Law which Moses gave to the Children of Israel"

march around the synagogue rostrum, singing joyful hymns in honor of the Torah, "Be glad and rejoice with the joy of the law."

As the solemn procession circles the synagogue auditorium the assembled kiss the garments of the scrolls, or touch the scrolls with their fingers and then kiss their fingers. This is Israel's token of love and reverence for the Word of God, beautiful in its original conception. But what a sad reflection as we think of Israel's spiritual reality!

There is something tragic about the people rejoicing over their most cherished possession, the Bible, dancing around with their noble, God-given and forgotten heritage.

Simchath Torah, the Rejoicing over the Law! Perhaps "The Feast of the Sealed Book" would be a more appropriate name, or the feast of a vision dimmed and wisdom departed.

How well do the words of Isaiah describe Israel's relation to the Bible.

"And the vision of all is become unto you as the words of a book that is sealed, which men deliver to one that is learned, saying, Read this, I pray thee: and he saith, I cannot; for it is sealed:

"And the book is delivered to him that is not learned . . . and he saith, I am not learned.

"Wherefore the Lord said, forasmuch as this people draw near me with their mouth, and with their lips do honour me, But have removed their heart far from me, and their fear toward me is taught by the precept of men:

"Therefore, the Lord said . . . behold, I will proceed to do a marvellous work among this people . . . the wisdom of their wise men shall perish, and the understanding of their prudent men shall be hid"—Isaiah 29:11-14.

Israel is yet waiting for her spiritual resurrection, when her eyes shall be opened by her Messiah Jesus, the seal broken, and her vision undimmed. Then shall her wisdom shine forth for her own healing and for the blessing of the nations. Then it will be Simchath Torah indeed, a true day of rejoicing. The people and The Book shall embrace each other, never to be separated.

Chapter Seven

Hanukkah—The Feast of Dedication and Christmas

"And it was at Jerusalem the feast of the dedication, and it was winter. And Jesus walked in the temple in Solomon's porch."
—John 10:22, 23

THIS is the only place in the New Testament where the Feast of Dedication, which the Jews call Hanukkah, is mentioned. This festival has been celebrated since the year 164 B.C. and continues to the present time. Hanukkah often coincides with Christmas which starts on the 25th of Kislev, the Jewish month which approximates our December. This identity of dates is more than a mere coincidence. The Feast of Hanukkah and Christmas, the birth of our Lord, are closely related, as we shall see later.

The Story Behind the Feast of Dedication

In the year 169 B.C. Antiochus Epiphanes, the Hellenized ruler of Syria (175-163 B.C.), a vile and godless man, campaigned against Egypt. Yet in spite of his victory he was compelled to withdraw from Egypt at the command of powerful Rome. At that time Palestine was under Syrian rule. Returning to Syria, Antiochus vented his wrath upon the hapless Judeans by entering Jerusalem, destroying a large part of the city, and slaughtering men, women and children. To crown his infamy, he invaded the Holy Temple, carrying away the golden altar, the candlesticks, the golden vessels, and other sacred treasures.

To show his contempt for Jehovah, he sacrificed a pig to the Greek god Jupiter. He also sternly forbade the Jews in the Holy Land and abroad to observe their religion, particularly the rite of circumcision, the observance of the Sabbath, and laws pertaining to clean animals.

He commanded that only pigs be sacrificed in the Temple of God. He himself cooked a pig in the Temple and poured its broth on the holy scrolls of the law and upon the altar, thus polluting it sacrilegiously.

Syrian officers and supervisors were dispatched into every city and village of Palestine to enforce the cruel and blasphemous decrees of Antiochus Epiphanes.

In terror many of the Jews fled to caves. Others, especially a number of Hellenized priests, cravenly complied with the Syrian ruler's commands. But there was a small minority of the faithful who dared defy "Antiochus the Wicked," as he became known in Jewish history.

"Who is on the Lord's Side?"

One day Apelles, an enforcement officer of Antiochus, arrived in the small township of Modin, three miles north of Jerusalem, and commanded the assembled Jews to sacrifice a swine. Mattathias (Matthew) the Maccabee, head of a priestly family faithful to the Lord, and father of five stalwarts, enraged by the ungodly decree, killed the first Jew about to

61

comply with the order. Then he and his five sons fell upon Apelles and his group of soldiers and killed them all.

This was the sign of an uprising of the Jews against the Syrians, their enemies, and the enemies of their God. Soon after Mattathias died, his son Judas the Maccabee, assembled a considerable number of courageous Jews and skilfully led them in battle against the Syrians.

Fired by the courage and devotion of Judas and his four brothers, the once timid and despairing now flocked to the side of their leader. They fought in the mountains and the valleys of Judea. They attacked the invaders guerilla fashion, giving them no respite. As they gained in strength, they ventured to face their enemies in open battle and defeated them.

Finally they drove the Syrians from Jerusalem, together with the disloyal priests who collaborated with the invaders. After cleansing the Holy Temple they demolished the polluted altar of God. Then on Kislev the 25th (December), 164 B.C., they rededicated the Temple of God amidst great rejoicing and consecrated a new altar in place of the old.

Only they did not know what to do with the stones of the old altar—sacred and precious to them, but at the same time polluted and unfit for the offering of sacrifices. So they decided to heap them together in a corner of the Temple and to wait for the coming of Elijah or Messiah to tell them what to do with these stones.

In the light of this the ancient query of the

Jews when they asked Jesus, "Art thou he that should come? or look we for another?" takes on a special significance. Also the statement of our Saviour, "Destroy this temple, and in three days I will raise it up." They were thinking of a temple made of stones and wood, while the Lord Jesus was referring to Himself, the Living Temple of God.

The Miracle of the Cruse of Oil

Hidden in one of the nooks of the Temple the Jews found a small jar of consecrated oil, used in former days for the perpetual light in the Temple. The oil was sufficient only for one night, but lo and behold the little cruse of oil lasted for eight days, until a new supply could be prepared and consecrated.

In memory of the wonderful redemption from the hands of the wicked enemy, and the rededication of the Temple, it was decreed that for eight days eight candles should be lit in every Jewish household, beginning with one on the first day, two on the second, progressively until the eighth day.

The Link

Now we turn to Christmas or the day when our Saviour was born. The Word of God does not give us any definite time when our Saviour was born. Maybe the Lord, in His wisdom did not see fit to reveal this to us, lest we confuse gaudy celebrations and merrymaking, the worship of the day rather than the One who is worthy of our worship, our love and our service.

It is interesting, however, to note that apparently the early Christians saw a vital link between the Feast of Dedication and the day when Christ was born. On the one hand a temple made with human hands—on the other, the Living Temple of God which came down from Heaven to dwell in our midst. For Christ compared Himself to that temple when He said, "Destroy this temple, and in three days I will raise it up"—John 2:19.

And so since the end of the third century, the 25th of December, which is, according to the Jewish calendar, the 25th of Kislev, and the generally accepted date for the Day of Hanukkah, has become Christmas.

Of course this date has never met with universal acceptance and from the early times of the church, even unto the present day, there have been dissensions and speculations as to which is the day when Christ was born.

The Light of the World

One day Jesus stood in the sanctuary watching the bright illumination which was a custom during the Feast of Tabernacles, and the Feast of Dedication. Looking at these lights He said, "I am the light of the world: he that followeth me shall not walk in darkness but shall have the light of life."

Today when the Jews kindle the Hanukkah lights they are careful to light each candle from the light known as the Servant, a beautiful symbol of Christ, the Servant of God—the Light of the World. He alone is able to kindle in our hearts the light of God. Only in His light can we see light.

Such briefly is the relationship between the Feast of Dedication of the Temple, and Christ, the Living Temple of God.

The symbol of Hanukkah is a candlestick with nine little candles. The flickering lights of nine little candles mean a great deal in the pitch darkness of night. But when the Sun arises then the candle light appears pale and insignificant. Thus to us Christ, the Sun of Righteousness, has dimmed the candle lights of Hanukkah. We thank God for these small lights during the darkness of the past night. But we go on to live in the daylight from on high.

Christmas the Great Jewish Festival

But even if we know little or nothing of the history of the Feast of Dedication, can any Christian fail to realize that in its very essence, the birth of our Saviour is rooted and grounded in the history of Israel? For He is God's answer to the promises He made to His people for a Messiah. It is God's answer to the yearnings of Israel for salvation, expressed in a thousand ways in Scripture.

Christ is the hope of Israel become a reality, a reality more glorious, more wonderful than any priest, prophet or seer ever envisioned.

"The people that walked in darkness have seen a great light: they that dwell in the land of the shadow of death, upon them hath the light shined.

"For unto us a child is born, unto us a son is given: and the government shall be upon his shoulder: and his name shall be called Wonderful, Counselor, the mighty God, the everlasting Father, the Prince of Peace.

"Of the increase of his government and peace there shall be no end, upon the throne of David, and upon his kingdom, to order it, and to establish it with judgment and with justice from henceforth even for ever. The zeal of the Lord of hosts will perform this"—Isaiah 9:2, 6,7.

Oh, how we long for the day when both the story of Hanukkah and the story of Christmas will be told in every Jewish home, side by side, and the glory of Christ shall dim all past victories and past glories, and He alone shall be the King of Glory in every heart.

"And so all Israel shall be saved: as it is written, there shall come out of Sion the Deliverer, and shall turn away ungodliness from Jacob."—Romans 11:26.

Chapter Eight

Purim—The Feast of Esther

He that Keepeth Israel

AMONG the Feasts of Israel, Purim, also known as the Feast of Esther, holds a much favored position. According to some of the rabbis, when Messiah shall come, all the feasts will become redundant, but Purim shall never cease.

This high esteem for Purim would be puzzling were it not for the fact that it is an expression of faith in the invisible working of an Invisible God behind the scenes of human events. The story of Esther is a fitting tribute to the God of an exiled people, without a temple or a priesthood, without a prophet or even a great spiritual leader, who nevertheless are deeply conscious of the divine watchcare upon them.

The Book of Esther so conspicuous by the absence of the name of God, seems to be shouting in its every line and word, "Behold, he that keepeth Israel shall neither slumber nor sleep."

Purim in Jewish Life

Purim comes on the 14th and 15th days of Adar, the twelfth month of the Bible year, approximately our March.

Every year during the Feast of Purim, the story of Esther is read with glee in the synagogues. Mordecai's name is cheered, and Haman's greeted with the stamping of the feet, with derisive booing, and the grinding sound of special noisemakers. Private and public merriment is in order. Gifts are sent to friends and to the poor, in a joyful reenactment of the first Purim, commemorating the deliverance of the Jews from the hands of their enemies, Haman and his henchmen.

As we read the story of Esther we notice an exquisite fabric of seeming coincidences woven by the invisible but sure hand of God into a pattern that spells deliverance. It has a lesson not only for the Jew, but also for all believers; that in the commonplace human events God moves to accomplish His plans. But it takes the eye of faith to see this.

The setting of the story is in ancient Persia at the peak of her power and glory. Some years have passed since Cyrus in 538 B.C. permitted the Jews to return from Babylon to the Holy Land, under the leadership of Zerubbabel (Ezra, chapters 1-6).

Those Jews who stayed behind in Babylon chose to live comfortably in dispersion rather than face the hardships of pioneering in their devastated homeland. Among those who decided to remain in exile we find Mordecai and Esther. Upon the throne of the Persian Empire, stretching over 127 provinces, sits Xerxes (486-465 B.C.), a mighty ruler of nations, but a weak character. His decisions are often engineered by sycophantic courtiers and intriguing politicians. The Jewish rabbis are fond of calling Ahasuerus, "a fool of a king," probably not without cause.

Yet behind the vacillation and the follies of a king, behind intrigues and political maneuvers of the royal court, there is God working out His eternal plans. It is fascinating to watch the divine hand behind the "perfectly natural" coincidences, weaving an intricate fabric to shield and to protect God's people.

Haman — the Tool of Satan

Haman, the evil spirit of the drama, is a descendant of Amalek, the eternal enemy of Israel, whom God commanded them to destroy utterly (Exodus 17:16). It was Saul, the first king of Israel, who disobeyed God and saved Haman's ancestors, thus bringing upon the children of Israel the dire peril of Haman. But watch the artistry of the divine providence choosing Mordecai of the same tribe and family as Saul, to repair the damage. For with the annihilation of Haman and his sons, the divine verdict to destroy Amalek has been carried out.

But Haman the prime minister and majordomo of Ahasuerus does not know these things. This vain-glorious politician obsessed with Jew hatred is tightening the noose around his neck without realizing it, for whom God would punish He first deprives of his reason.

Haman was a tool of Satan who from the beginning of time sought to destroy the Jews. Satan knew that out of Abraham's seed should come the One who would bruise his head.

Haman's reaction to Mordecai is perfectly modern. The Jew Mordecai, has offended Haman, and so Haman's wrath turns against all the Jews. Historic patterns have a way of repeating themselves.

A Bill of Indictment

When Haman comes to Ahasuerus requesting the total extirpation of the Jews he has a readymade bill of particulars against them. This bill of indictment is worth our analysis:

"And Haman said unto King Ahasuerus, there is a certain people scattered abroad and dispersed among the people in all the provinces of thy kingdom; and their laws are diverse from all people; neither keep they the king's laws: therefore it is not for the king's profit to suffer them" (Esther 3:8).

These accusations are historic because they have been levelled against the Jew repeatedly throughout his checkered and tragic history.

1. "The Jews are a people scattered abroad and dispersed among all the people." The charge is that the Jews are an alien element in the body of the host nation.

2. "They have divers laws." Their religion and their customs, the whole structure of their society and civilization do not fit into the pattern of the host country, is the next indictment.

3. "They do not obey the king's laws." A charge of disloyalty and lack of patriotism.

Finally and summing it all up—"It benefited not the king to suffer them." They are a burden on the body politic and on the economy of the land. And so they are useless to the king, and the country is better off without them. Said Solomon the Wise, "There is nothing new under the sun."

A Drastic Solution

"If it please the king, let it be written that they may be destroyed." Haman like Hitler and countless others, has a ready solution to the Jewish problem—destroy the Jews, total extermination.

70

Haman is not unaware of the economic value of the Jew to the country. He realizes that their absence might hit the king where it hurts. So he offers as a compensation the tidy sum of 10,000 talents of silver (some forty to fifty million dollars in our somewhat inflated currency) "into the hands of those who have charge of the king's treasury." Apparently Haman did not do so badly as a high government official in those remote days in "Shushan, D.C." However, Ahasuerus magnanimously refused to accept the offer and gave Haman the Jews anyway. "Do with them as you like".

How often were the Jews delivered to the mercy of the merciless! Now the verdict has been pronounced, the trap set. Is there any escape for the hunted?

When Kings and Captains Drink

"The king and Haman sat down to drink—but the city Shushan was perplexed." These few words in a masterful way describe the tragedy of the situation. The king and his chief advisor sat down to drink, while Shushan was perplexed.

Woe to a country where rulers indulge in revelry while their subjects are perplexed. There is something very tragic and ominous in such a state of affairs and divine retribution cannot be far delayed.

A Remedy Which Brings Results

But man's extremity is God's opportunity. Night is darkest before dawn. Upon hearing the decree, the first reaction of the Jews was to fast, pray and repent. What a wholesome example to follow! A sure remedy which has never failed to move the heart of God. For it is He who promised:

"If my people, which are called by my name, shall humble themselves, and pray, and seek my face, and turn from their wicked ways; then will I hear from heaven, and will forgive their sin, and will heal their land" (2 Chronicles 7:14).

Queen Esther

Meet Esther, first Lady of the great Persian Empire, elevated from a humble Jewish maiden to the position of queen, by the strange workings of God's design.

Esther and Mordecai show indications of trying hard to obliterate their Jewish background. Their very presence in Persia suggests that they had chosen the comfort of Persia rather than the hardships of the Holy Land.

Significantly, their names are not Jewish, but rather of Babylonian origin. The name "Mordecai" is believed to be a variant of "Merodach" the name of the patron deity of Babylon, mentioned in Jeremiah 50:2. And Esther is strangely reminiscent of the Babylonian goddess Ishtar or Astarte. The effort to assimilate themselves to their environment has often been repeated in Jewish history. In speech, manner, dress and by their very names, the Jews have often sought to take on the coloring of the people among whom they lived, but in the final analysis with little avail. When the hour struck God always sent the Hamans and the Hitlers to remind them through blood and through tears of their origin and of their destiny.

There may have been much antagonism against the Jews in the Persian Empire at the time, for Esther's close relative and adoptive father, Mordecai, found it necessary to advise her not to betray her Jewish nationality to the king or to the court. Latent anti-Semitism probably was deepseated among the people of the Persian Empire, so that Haman found a ready and even eager audience for his Jew-hatred. The Hamans and the Hitlers are only possible where latent hatreds are already pent up in the hearts of the masses. And so Esther guarded the secret of her Jewish descent well—too well. Mordecai found it necessary to remind his exalted relative:

"Think not with thyself that thou shalt escape in the king's house, more than all the Jews"—Esther 4:13.

Beautiful Esther, queen of the royal household, afraid to show her colors while her people perish! What a striking picture of a child of God rejoicing in his own salvation and at ease while men and women for whom we ought to be burdened and concerned—perish.

But when the time strikes, God always sends a deliverer—a Moses in the wilderness; a Samson when the Philistines roam; a Judas Maccabeus when the godless Syrians flood the land and threaten to destroy God's people; a Mordecai and Esther when a sinister Persian seeks to exterminate the "everlasting people."

When the need arises God has someone specially appointed to come into the kingdom in order to deal with the peril of the hour.

"For if thou altogether holdest thy peace at this time, then shall there enlargement and deliverance arise to the Jews from another place; but thou and thy father's house shall be destroyed: and who knoweth whether thou art come to the kingdom for such a time as this?" Esther 4:14.

Christian, the Lord has called you into His kingdom for a purpose. He has a special task for you, a precious privilege peculiarly your own. Are you willing to follow His leading, or does the Lord have to replace you with an instrument more yielded to His will? God will bring about His purpose, but you may be passed by.

Esther's determination and devotion are a beautiful testimony for all children of God to follow. "If I perish, I perish." It is only men and women who are willing to lay down their lives in the cause of God, whom the Lord can use gloriously. It is not so much gifts and abilities, but the perfect yieldedness in which the Lord delights.

Shilly-shallying and half-heartedness cannot prosper or be blessed. We remember our Saviour's words, "So then because thou art lukewarm, and neither cold nor hot, I will spue thee out of my mouth" (Revelation 3:16).

Anti-Semitism, A Blinding Obsession

We watch Haman basking in the honors bestowed upon him by his lord and master, Ahasuerus. He relates to his wife and friends the dignities already bestowed upon him, and gleefully anticipates honors yet to come. But the fly in Haman's ointment is Mordecai, the Jew, the obstinate Jew with the unbending knee. O, if only he could get rid of Mordecai, his bliss would be unmarred. And Mordecai the Jew becomes Haman's obsession. An obsession not uncommon among many otherwise reasonable and intelligent people. When you speak to them they are rational, as long as you do not touch the subject of the Jew. But mention the Jew and they see red.

The Jew in their imagination is behind everything. All their own personal problems and frustrations, all international complexities and human woes, all that ever went wrong, is due to the Jew—the serpent in the fool's paradise.

A Bit of Divine Irony

There is a bit of divine irony in the story of Haman. He who plans and schemes against the destruction of the Jew invokes divine wrath against himself. Haman in his blindness and in pursuit of his own aggrandizement unknowingly sets the stage for Mordecai's promotion and for his own humiliation and final destruction. He seeks to hang Mordecai, but the very gallows which he erects for Mordecai are destined to destroy its designer.

Haman is only one in the long procession of men whom God has raised up to confirm the truth of His Word. "No weapon that is formed against thee (the Jews) shall prosper" (Isaiah 54:17).

"... And hate thine enemies"

The book of Esther has often been the pretext for severe criticism even among Christians (Luther). The Jews, the critics said, are revengeful and unforgiving. In this matter we would like to make one or two basic observations.

First, let us remember that we are dealing with a people in a pre-Christian dispensation. The Gospel of forgiveness and love has not been made known to them. It is a dispensation of retribution, and laws of severe justice prevail —a life for a life and an eye for an eye. A man who does not take two eyes for one eye is considered righteous. It was our Saviour Himself who reminded his listeners:

"Ye have heard that it has been said, Thou shalt love thy neighbor, and hate thine enemy."

Such was the spirit of the time in which the drama of Mordecai and Esther was enacted. It is only in the light of the times and the revelation given to the people that we may judge them.

The natural man hates his enemies and when he loves his friends this is considered to be a great virtue. Only our Saviour prayed upon the cross to which His enemies nailed Him, "Father forgive them; for they know not what they do" (Luke 23:34).

The second point to be considered is that Esther asked for the right of self-defense for her people. This was granted to them and when the appointed hour for their destruction came, they had the privilege and encouragement of the king to stand in their own defense. Of this they availed themselves, not unwillingly. Yet they were specially careful not to take any spoil from their defeated enemies, lest the stigma of robbery attach itself to them.

And So We Have Purim

In commemoration of that great deliverance, Mordecai and Esther instituted the Feast of Purim, which means "lots." "Wherefore they called these days Purim after the name Pur"— Esther 9:26. The idolatrous and superstitious Haman decided to find out which would be the propitious day to destroy the Jews and so he cast lots. The lot fell upon the 13th day of Adar, the twelfth month in God's calendar.

And so the day of destruction and appointed defeat turned into a day of deliverance for the Jews. In the last analysis, their victory is the victory of God over Satan, the victory of prayer, fasting, and faith over pagan wrath and blind hatred. It is the victory of the Providence and lovingkindness of Jehovah, who neither sleeps nor slumbers.

Purim, like the preceding Feast of Hanukkah, is a link in the chain of preservation and redemption which God Himself has forged for His people. Purim is a signpost on the road of salvation, ascending from physical deliverance to the perfect redemption, which only the Lord Jesus Christ can give to them who accept His sacrifice upon the Cross of Calvary.

The partial, imperfect, physical deliverance which God has wrought through Mordecai points to Christ, who is able to save to the uttermost.

"Wherefore the law was our schoolmaster to bring us unto Christ" (Galatians 3:24).

Chapter Nine

Sabbath The Queen

The sun has disappeared beyond the trees
Let us go forth to greet Sabbath the Queen
Behold she comes, the holy and blest,
And with her the angels of peace and rest.
Come in, come in, Blessed Queen,
Peace be unto you too, you angels of peace.

Israel's Exclusive Heritage

FOR generations untold, the Sabbath has been to the Jew the Queen and Bride of the soul, a God-appointed day of rest and worship.

The Sabbath is deeply imbedded in the heart of Judaism, a pivotal point of Jewish life. Sabbath and circumcision are the two distinguishing marks of Judaism. None can be thought of as a truly religious Jew in the rabbinical sense unless he observes both.

"Sabbath" means rest. It is preeminently and distinctly a Jewish holiday, given by God to the Children of Israel through His servant Moses on the Mount of Sinai.

"And the Lord spake unto Moses, saying, Speak thou also unto the children of Israel, saying, Verily my sabbaths ye shall keep: for it is a sign between me and you throughout your generations; that ye may know that I am the Lord that doth sanctify you.

Ye shall keep the sabbath therefore; for it is holy unto you; every one that defileth it shall surely be put to death: for whosoever doeth any work therein, that soul shall be cut off from among his people"—Exodus 31:12-14.

The Sabbath is exclusively Israel's heritage, given under the law—to the people of the law. The observance of the Sabbath as originally ordained by God presupposes the existence of a holy Temple, a God-appointed Priesthood, and a sacrificial system.

"And on the sabbath day two lambs of the first year without spot, and two tenth deals of flour for a meat-offering, mingled with oil, and the drink-offering thereof:

This is the burnt-offering of every sabbath, beside the continual burnt-offering, and his drink-offering"—Numbers 28:9, 10.

The Sabbath Observed in Breach Only

As things stand today, a Jew cannot observe the Sabbath in its Scriptural setting, because the essential conditions for such observances are absent. What the Jews of today try to observe is the rabbinical version of the Sabbath. But this much-changed Sabbath is even more impossible of strict observance for the following reasons:

The vast majority of the Jews simply are unfamiliar with the intricate system of rabbinical law, without the knowledge of which it is impossible to keep the Sabbath.

The Rabbis always sought to make the breaking of the Torah (the Law) as difficult as possible. To achieve it they built up what they called a "Fence around the Law." They made injunctions and regulations prohibiting things which God Himself never forbade. It is as if the United States Congress, in an effort to keep inviolate the gold of Fort Knox, would forbid anyone even to approach the state boundaries of Kentucky. Anyone setting foot on the soil of Kentucky would be considered as if he actually broke in and robbed the gold of Fort Knox.

The recorded teachings of these ancient Rabbis (approximately second to fifth century A.D.) are know as the Talmud. The Talmud is a collection of Scripture commentaries, folk lore, a treasury of legendary and historical material and the record of legal discussions pertaining to all aspects of Jewish life. One of its treatises is called "Sabbath" and deals with matters related to the observance of Sabbath.

1521 Sabbath Rules

In the treatise "Sabbath," the Rabbis established 39 categories of activities which must not be performed on the Sabbath. These categories of forbidden activities are called Aboth, or "Fathers." In turn these main 39 categories are

Children kindling Sabbath Lights

subdivided into 39 classes which are called Toledoth, or "Offsprings," making a total of 39 x 39, or 1521 Sabbath rules.

The most simple and trivial matter of daily occurrence is the subject of involved disputes and ingenious Rabbinical legislation. We venture to say that not one Jew in a thousand knows them all even approximately.

The preparation of food for the Sabbath constitutes a vast and complicated subject of discussion and rabbinical ingenuity. All travel on the Sabbath, even to a synagogue service, is forbidden. The kindling of fire and even the turning on or off of electric lights is prohibited. Also writing of any kind is forbidden, etc., etc.

Such questions are discussed at great length: How far may a man walk on the Sabbath Day? What may he carry on the Sabbath Day without breaking the law of not bearing burdens? What is a burden? Is carrying of a handkerchief a burden? The answer if yes, if it is in the pocket; but no, if it is tied around the neck and thus used as a piece of apparel.

The Genius of Hairsplitting

The question of whether an egg laid on the Sabbath Day is fit for consumption constitutes the subject of a very learned and involved discussion. These and thousands of other questions are most seriously and learnedly discussed by great Rabbis, whom men call "sages," or "wise men."

These "wise men" erected fences and hedges around the Law and then turned around and showed how they may be circumvented. In this way they created a veritable system of prohibitions and evasions.

The Rabbis themselves seem to have been aware of the flimsy structure of their injunctions and prohibitions. One of them rightly observed: "Some of the laws of the Sabbath are like mountains suspended on a hair" (Chagigah 10a).

Here we have a bewildering example of where man's wisdom leads without the inspiration of the Holy Spirit. Manmade "religion" is not necessarily a blessing.

"For it is written, I will destroy the wisdom of the wise, and will bring to nothing the understanding of the prudent.

"For after that in the wisdom of God the world by wisdom knew not God, it pleased God by the foolishness of preaching to save them that believe"—1 Corinthians 1:19. 21.

Human wisdom unaided by the Holy Spirit invariably leads to lifeless sterility—busy windmills grinding no grain and providing no bread whereby man can live.

Let us not for a moment single out for condemnation the rabbis, those "great masters of little things." Parallel developments have taken place also in other religions, both in pagan as well as so-called "Christian." For example the scholastic theology of the Medieval Church has no occasion to envy the learned rabbis. Its theologians, too, created what might be called "A Christian Talmud."

A disputation concerning the question of how many demons can dance on the point of a needle (by a learned monk) is by no means more inspiring than the discussion by some learned rabbi, whether it be permissible on the Sabbath to wipe the mud off one's shoes.

The average Jew of today absorbed in the

cares of life has neither the time nor the inclination to study these things. And even if he did, the very effort to observe these laws, especially under modern conditions, would constitute a burden impossible of fulfillment. Nevertheless in spite of all that, devout Jews have tried to observe the Sabbath and have done it with great joy.

Seven is Sacred

Seven is a hallowed number in Scripture. The Lord created the world in six days and sanctified the seventh day as a day of rest— Sabbath.

Even as the seventh day is dedicated to God, so is the seventh month. It is the month of holy assemblies and seasons.

The New Year of the Jews falls on the first day of the seventh month, a day when God commanded a holy convocation, a day of rest and repentance, a day of sounding of the ram's horn.

The tenth day of the seventh month is the solemn Day of Atonement. The fifteenth day of the seventh month is the beginning of the eight day Feast of Tabernacles.

The Seventh Year is also sacred unto God, a Sabbatical year: "Six years thou shalt sow thy field, and six years thou shalt prune thy vineyard, and gather in the fruit thereof;
But the seventh year shall be a sabbath of rest unto the land, a sabbath for the Lord: thou shalt neither sow thy field, nor prune thy vineyard" —Leviticus 25:3, 4.

The Year of Jubilee

When seven Sabbatical years had been completed, the fiftieth year was a Year of Jubilee.

"And thou shalt number seven sabbaths of years unto thee, seven times seven years; and the space of the seven sabbaths of years shall be unto thee forty and nine years.

Then shalt thou cause the trumpet of the jubile to sound on the tenth day of the seventh month, in the day of atonement shall ye make the trumpet sound throughout all your land.

And ye shall hallow the fiftieth year, and proclaim liberty throughout all the land unto all the inhabitants thereof: it shall be a jubile unto you; and ye shall return every man unto his possession, and ye shall return every man unto his family.

In the year of this jubile ye shall return every man unto his possession"—Leviticus 25: 8-10, 13.

The Year of Jubilee is one of the most wonderful provisions which God made for His people, reflecting His great mercy and love. In the Year of Jubilee "the brother who had

A Knotty Point

84

waxed poor" had the opportunity to receive back his possessions lost through poverty, after making fair arrangements with the man who came into possession of the property belonging to the impoverished brother.

"If thy brother be waxed poor, and hath sold away some of his possession, and if any of his kin come to redeem it, then shall he redeem that which his brother sold"—Leviticus 25:25.

So also were all Hebrew servants to be set free. An Israelite was to be no man's servant, but God's.

Sabbath Today

With the continuous corrosion of religious life, the Sabbath observance has become more and more neglected. Some care not and some are simply forced by economic conditions to work or trade on the Sabbath like on any other day. Some Reformed Jews observe Sunday as their day of rest in keeping with the social pattern of life in the West. But a considerable number of Jews still try to observe the Sabbath according to rabbinical injunctions.

Since we have pointed out some rabbinical foibles, it is only fair that we also mention something that is good and wholesome in their teaching. Much of what the Rabbis thought still reflected the spirit of the Word of God, its righteousness and its mercy. Since the Sabbath Day is to be a day of rejoicing they encourage the providing of good things not only for their own families, but also for the poor and the stranger:

"And when he eats (the Jew) and drinks, he is bound to feed the stranger, the orphan, and the widow, with the poor. But he that bolts the doors of his house, and eats and drinks with his children and his wife, but does not furnish meat and drink to the poor and afflicted, is not to be regarded as having fulfilled the commandment; on the contrary, his joy is that of a glutton, and of such persons it is said, 'Their sacrifices shall be unto them as the bread of mourners; all that eat thereof shall be polluted; for their bread for their soul shall not come into the house of the Lord'—Hosea 9:4 (Arbah Turim, 529)."

The Beauty of Holiness

The Sabbath even when marred by human distortion still casts a glow on the family life of the observant Jew. Man has not been able to obliterate altogether some of the Heavenly beauty which the Lord has instilled into the Sabbath Day, which He has sanctified and made holy.

Like all other religious holidays, the Sabbath begins at sunset of the preceding day, that is on Friday evening. There is a service in the synagogue which consists of special prayers of welcome for the Sabbath, the Bride and Queen. The home is festively decorated, the tables decked, candles lit, and a special holiday supper is prepared for the family after they return home from the synagogue. A cup of wine is blessed and distributed among the members of the family. This is known as "Kiddush," which means sanctification.

After the supper a prayer of thanksgiving for the food is said and hymns of praise in honor of the Sabbath are chanted.

"Crown of days, above all blest
The Rock of Ages chose thee for His rest.

Six days are for toil created
But the seventh God has consecrated.

Do no labour! Thus He bade us
In six days a world He made us.
Crown of days, above all blest
The Rock of Ages chose thee for His rest."

Some of the hymns have definite Messianic overtones like the following:

"Elijah the Prophet
Elijah the Tishbite
Elijah the Gileadite
Come quickly to us
And bring the Messiah the Son of David"

The devotion of the Jew through the ages to the Sabbath has been something beautiful and heroic. It has set them apart from the Gentile world and has been a testimony and challenge

A Sabbath Afternoon in Tel Aviv

not only to the pagans but to Christians as well. Like circumcision, the Sabbath has helped to preserve the identity of the Jews and the very life of the Jewish people.

One of the Jewish thinkers, Achad Ha-am, has truly observed:

"Even more than the Jews have kept the Sabbath, has the Sabbath kept the Jews."

But what about the Christian? Is he under obligations to keep the Sabbath? Should he keep Sunday as the Lord's Day or the Sabbath of the Jews? How should he keep it? Is Sunday a "papal" invention, as some maintain?

Chapter Ten

Sabbath or The Lord's Day— Which?

THE subject of Sabbath versus Sunday observance presents one of the most heated controversies not only between Synagogue and Church, but within the Church itself, causing considerable confusion even among believers. It will be our effort to try to turn some light on the subject from the Word of God and from the earliest records of the Christian Church.

"Why do thy disciples not keep the Sabbath?" was one of the chief reproaches of the Jewish elders and the Pharisees against our Lord and His disciples. Yet our Lord in defending the deeds of love and healing which He performed on the Sabbath Day, and the plucking of the ears of corn by His hungry disciples, did not reject the observance of the Sabbath as such. What He did repudiate was the heavy burdens which the Rabbis imposed upon the people, man-made impositions, not based on the authority of the Word of God. He who was the Son of God was by virtue of His Messiahship also the Lord of the Sabbath.

"For the Son of Man is Lord even of the sabbath day"—Matthew 12:8.

But as long as our Saviour was in the flesh He lived under the law into which He was born. The Crucified and Risen Saviour fulfilled the whole purpose of the law.

"But when the fulness of the time was come, God sent forth his Son, made of a woman, made under the law, to redeem them that were under the law, that we might receive the adoption of sons"—Galatians 4:4, 5.

The law came to show men what God required of them, but Christ came to bring the grace which enables them to do the will of God.

The law was given to the Jews as a people, and the Sabbath together with circumcision were the foremost signs of God's covenant with Israel. The law of Moses was not intended for the Gentiles.

The early Christian church into which many Gentile believers had come was beset by strife and problems centering around the observance or non-observance of the ceremonial and ritual law. Even today the Church is still vexed by some of these problems. As of old, so even today some insist on keeping the Sabbath. Paul warns the believers against such:

"Ye are circumcised with the circumcision made without hands, in putting off the body of the sins of the flesh by the circumcision of Christ:

Let no man therefore judge you in meat, or in drink, or in respect of an holyday, or of the new moon, or of the sabbath days:

Which are a shadow of things to come; but the body is Christ"—Colossians 2:11, 16, 17.

The Apostle Paul clearly indicates that the Sabbath does not apply to the Christian, but only to the Jew who lived under the dispensation of the law of Moses. In the previous chapter we have pointed out that even the Jew finds it impossible to keep the Sabbath in all its stringency. How much less can the Gentile hope to keep it effectively? The law only serves to emphasize our helplessness in the face of God's command and squarely throws us upon the mercy and grace of God.

Significantly the Jewish Rabbis themselves have always thought of the Sabbath as being exclusively the privilege of Israel, basing this on Exodus 31:12-17.

Because of this they resented any Gentile attempt to keep the Sabbath or any other part of the law, without complete submission to the law in its entirety. The following words give expression to their sentiments:

"A Gentile who employs himself in the law is guilty of death. Thus a Gentile who keeps a Sabbath, though it be on one of the week days, if he make it to himself as a Sabbath, he is guilty of death. Either let a Gentile become a proselyte of righteousness (a convert to Judaism) and take upon him the whole law: or let him remain in his own law, and neither add nor diminish. But if he employs himself in the law, or keeps a Sabbath, or makes any innovation, he is to be beaten and punished, and informed that he for this is guilty of death, but he is not to be killed"—Hilchoth Melachim, chapter 10:9.

The Difference Between the Sabbath and the Lord's Day

There are basic differences between the Sabbath of the Jew and the Lord's Day which we need to bear always in mind:

1. The Sabbath or the seventh day of the week commemorates a completed physical creation—Genesis 2:1-3.

The first day of the week is the day of

resurrection and signifies a completed redemption—Matthew 28:1-6.

2. The Sabbath is a covenant sign between God and His people Israel.

"Speak thou also unto the children of Israel, saying, verily my sabbaths ye shall keep: for it is a sign between me and you throughout your generations; that ye may know that I am the Lord that doth sanctify you"—Exodus 31:13.

The first day of the week signifies the fellowship between the Church and her Lord.

"And upon the first day of the week, when the disciples came together to break bread, Paul preached unto them, ready to depart on the morrow"—Acts 20:7.

3. The Sabbath observance was commanded by the law. The punishment for non-compliance was death.

"Ye shall keep the sabbath therefore; for it is holy unto you; everyone that defileth it shall surely be put to death: for whosoever doeth any work therein, that soul shall be cut off from among his people"—Exodus 31:14.

The Lord's Day is a day of voluntary, spontaneous worship without any commandment— a day of witness and labor for the Lord.

4. The Sabbath is an essential part of the covenant of works. The Lord's Day is representative of the covenant of grace.

5. The Sabbath is the crowning day of the week which rewards man for his toil. The Lord's Day emphasizes what God has done for man through His only begotten Son.

It is significant that all the commandments of the Decalogue are mentioned in one or another form throughout the New Testament as a moral code which applies to the believer whether he be Jew or Gentile. But there is one exception, the fourth commandment, the keeping of the Sabbath, which is nowhere commanded in the New Testament.

The Parting Was Painful

The Jewish believer in Christ was in a dilemma from the very beginning. Eventually it forced him out of the synagogue into a fellowship which was distinctly Christian, the ecclesia.

The dilemma of the Jewish Christian was this. By the ties of blood and by the affection of his heart, he felt himself to be an integral part of Israel. He differed, however, from his unbelieving brethen by his faith in the Lord, the Messiah Jesus, to whom he owed supreme allegiance. For some time after the Resurrection the Jewish believers still attended the Temple worship in Jerusalem.

"And they, continuing daily with one accord in the temple, and breaking bread from house to house." Acts 2:46.

Nevertheless the separation between believers and unbelievers was soon forced upon the Christians by violence and persecution. The first martyr for the faith was Stephen. Active persecution of Jewish believers, the vilification of the person of the Lord Jesus, and changes in the liturgy, which contained direct or implicit denunciation of the believers in the Messiah Jesus, drove the Jewish Christians out of the Temple and the synagogue.

To the daily prayers of the synagogue was added the "Birkath-Hamminim," "The blessing of the Sectarians," which was in reality a malediction. This is how the strange "blessing" was worded in the original Hebrew version: "And for the Apostates let there be no hope, and the dominion of arrogance (probably Rome —Editor's note) may it be speedily uprooted in our days. Let the Nazarenes (Jewish Christians) and the Sectarians perish as in a moment. May they be blotted out from the Book of Life and with the Righteous ones may they not be inscribed. Blessed art thou Jehovah, who humblest the arrogant."

Today this prayer in a considerably changed form is used in the synagogue. But the word "Apostates" has been changed to "Slanderers," and the direct reference to the Nazarenes and the Sectarians is omitted. Obviously a Jewish

Upper Jordan in Galilee

Christian could not stay on in the synagogue where his Lord was calumniated and he himself made the subject of malediction.

If the Gospel was not to be confined to the narrow territorial and spiritual boundaries of Judea, the breach had to come, so that the Gospel of salvation might have free course not only among the Jews, but also among the nations.

"As for Saul, he made havock of the church, entering into every house, and haling men and women committed them to prison.

Therefore they that were scattered abroad went everywhere preaching the word"—Acts 8:3, 4.

The final breach took place in the times of the false Messiah, Bar Kochba, who fought against the Romans and died in battle 135 A.D. The Jewish believers could not endorse his claims nor support his warfare. Believers had to leave Jerusalem and eventually Palestine. Henceforth the Church and the synagogue went separate paths. The daughter was forcibly weaned from her mother.

The First Christians and the Sabbath Question

At first Jewish believers apparently continued for some time in the voluntary observance of the Sabbath, not because they felt their salvation rested upon this, but rather out of regard for the sensibilities of their own people.

At the same time they felt the inner need to assemble themselves on the day of our Saviour's triumph, His Resurrection, and to break bread and to remember His death and coming again. Prayers were offered and the Word preached

(Acts 20). After the early Jewish church was scattered abroad and the majority of believers were from among the Gentiles, the Sabbath observance soon came into disuse.

The early church was faced with a fierce struggle. There were two imcompatible groups. One representing the Judaizing element of the Church who believed that a Gentile in order to become a Christian must first become a Jew and conform to all the Law of Moses.

Opposed to these were the main fellowship of the Christian Church, those who believed that Gentile believers were under no such obligation to the Law.

The New Testament, especially the Acts of the Apostles, and Paul's Epistles to the Galatians and to the Colossians, vividly depict this struggle. The matter came to a head at the first Christian Synod in Jerusalem—Acts 15.

The Apostle James, the first bishop of Jerusalem, presided, (not St. Peter—the alleged first pope) and gave the following ruling: "Forasmuch as we have heard, that certain which went out from us have troubled you with words, subverting your souls, saying, ye must be circumcised, and keep the law: to whom we gave no such commandment.

For it seemed good to the Holy Ghost, and to us, to lay upon you no greater burden than these necessary things; That ye abstain from meats offered to idols, and from blood, and from things strangled, and from fornication: from which if ye keep yourselves, ye shall do well. Fare ye well"—Acts 15:24, 28, 29.

The imposition of the Sabbath upon the Gentile believers is conspicuous by its absence —not a word about it.

After that First Synod in Jerusalem Paul devoted all his energy in defense of the Gospel of Grace against all those who would impose the legal system of Moses as a necessity for Gentile believers. His heart agonized when he saw the confusion and the deadening effects of the Judaizing teachings upon the Gentile converts. Here is a typical passage which gives us a glimpse into Paul's heart:

"O foolish Galatians, who hath bewitched you, that ye should not obey the truth, before whose eyes Jesus Christ hath been evidently set forth, crucified among you?

This only would I learn of you, Received ye the Spirit by the works of the law, or by the hearing of faith?

For as many as are of the works of the law are under the curse: for it is written, Cursed is every one that continueth not in all things which are written in the book of the law.

But that no man is justified by the law in the sight of God, it is evident: for, The just shall live by faith"—Galatians 3:1, 2, 10, 11.

"For in Christ Jesus neither circumcision availeth any thing, nor uncircumcision, but a new creature"—Galatians 6:15.

To cling to the Sabbath was for Paul to cling to the beggarly elements—to exchange the glorious reality in Christ for the mere shadow which the Law of Moses represents.

The main body of the Church consisting both of Jew and Gentiles very early began to observe the first day of the week as "The Lord's Day." There were, however, some Jews who persisted in the observance of the Sabbath as well as of other rites of the ceremonial law. They had no fellowship with the other Christians who did not observe the law.

These Judaizing Hebrew believers, called Nazarenes and Ebionites, cut off from the main flow of Christian life and fellowship within the Church and despised also by the synagogue, in time vanished from the horizon. They were eventually swallowed up by Judaism or gnosticism.

The historical record of the early Christians indicates clearly that the First Day became the Christian day of worship—the Lord's Day.

"And upon the first day of the week, when the disciples came together to break bread, Paul preached unto them, ready to depart on the morrow; and continued his speech until midnight"—Acts 20:7.

Barnabas, one of the Apostolic Fathers of the First Century A.D., writes: "We keep the Lord's Day with joyfulness, the day on which Jesus rose from the dead."

The "Didache of the Apostles," one of the earliest Christian documents also of the First Century, which contained the teachings of the Apostles, states:

"On the Lord's own day gather yourselves together and break bread and give thanks."

Ignatius, Bishop of Antioch, in the year 110 A.D., says: "Those who walked in the ancient practices attain unto newness of hope, no longer observing sabbaths, but fashioning their lives after the Lord's Day, on which our life also rose through Him, that we may be found disciples of Jesus Christ, our only teacher."

Justin Martyr, in the year 135 A.D., says: "Sunday is the day on which we all hold common assembly, because it is the first day on which God having wrought a change in the darkness and matter made the world, and Jesus Christ our Saviour on the same day rose from the dead. And on the day called Sunday all who live in cities or in the country gather together to one place and the memoirs of the Apostles or the writings of the prophets are read as long as time permits."

These are just a few of the historic documents of the early Church relating to the subject.

To maintain as some do that the observance of the first day of the week as the Lord's Day was instituted by the Popes or Constantine the Great in the fourth century, is to betray a basic ignorance of New Testament facts and to fly in the face of the recorded history of the Christian Church. What happened is that Constantine the Great, so-called, upon accepting Christianity, enacted in 321 A.D. the first "Sunday Law," making for the Roman Empire the Sunday observance obligatory. But that was already the practice of Christians since the days of the Apostles.

The Sabbath Versus Sunday Issue

The Jews of the Western world often find themselves in a peculiar predicament. Their Gentile neighbors work on the Sabbath and take Sunday off for worship, if believers; or pleasure, if unbelievers.

The Jew closely integrated in the economic and social pattern of life, is forced often to work on the Sabbath and to relax on Sunday. If he is to worship at all he may have to do it on Sunday. It has therefore become a practice at least among some reformed Jews to hold "Sabbath" services on Sunday.

Conversely Jewish Christians in Israel are faced with the same problem in reverse—observing "Sunday" on Saturday.

In the new State of Israel the believers live in a Jewish economy. The Sabbath is the legal day of rest. Sunday is a work day like every other day. Most believers are therefore unable to foregather on Sunday and consequently have to worship the Lord, attend services and pray on the Sabbath. To insist that the Hebrew Christian should not work on Sunday would mean to jeopardize his already precarious existence. Shall we judge him for that?

The position of the Hebrew Christian today closely parallels that of his believing ancestors of the early Church. We could not do better than follow the Apostle Paul who gives us very clear guidance in this matter.

"One man esteemeth one day above another: another esteemeth every day alike. Let every man be fully persuaded in his own mind.

He that regardeth the day, regardeth it unto the Lord; and he that regardeth not the day, to the Lord he doth not regard it. He that eateth, eateth to the Lord, for he giveth God thanks; and he that eateth not, to the Lord he eateth not, and giveth God thanks.

For none of us liveth to himself, and no man dieth to himself"—Rom. 14:5-7.

The keeping of the Lord's Day dedicated to divine worship and witness is a godly, wholesome, and altogether commendable practice, refreshing for the body, and quickening to the spirit. Furthermore it is based on the example and practice of the first Christians according to Scriptural and post-Scriptural testimony.

Yet our salvation does not rest upon the

observance of any particular day, be it Saturday or Sunday. The point in all these matters which we must bear in mind is this: our salvation rests entirely and uncompromisingly on the finished work of Calvary. Salvation is what the Lord has done and not what we do. We can neither add nor subtract, only accept it in faith.

In the State of Israel the Jewish believer may wish out of loyalty to his people to observe the Sabbath, or to practice circumcision, or to refuse to eat pork. So long as he does not make this a question of salvation it matters little. Said the Apostle Paul: "Unto the Jews I became as a Jew, that I might gain the Jews"—1 Corinthians 9:20.

A Rest to the People of God

The Lord's Day is a day of spiritual rest. Not a day of idleness, nor of man-enforced prohibitions, but a day when "peace like a river" floods the soul.

This kind of Sabbath is unknown to the Jew, but it is the blessed experience and heritage of the child of God who has found rest and peace in the Messiah of the Jews, the Lord Jesus Christ. "There remaineth therefore a rest (a Sabbath) to the people of God.
For he that is entered into his rest, he also hath ceased from his own works, as God did from his. Let us labour therefore to enter into that rest, lest any man fall after the same example of unbelief"—Hebrews 4:9-11.

The Liberty Wherewith Christ Has Made Us Free

Those of us who have been raised under the Law know the deadening effect of the Law.

101

"The letter killeth but the spirit giveth life." How pathetic and misguided are some Christians who would induce anyone, Jew or Gentile, who has known "the liberty wherewith Christ has made us free" to take upon themselves again the burden of the Law. With the Apostle Paul, we feel like saying: "O, foolish Galatians, who hath bewitched you?"

Years ago in Poland when I was a little Jewish boy of about five years, I remember "the Melamed," the teacher of religion, as he led by the hand little recalcitrant boys to "Cheder," the religious school of instruction. There the children were taught the Hebrew alphabet and the rudiments of The Scriptures. The Apostle Paul had a very similar picture in mind when he said, "Wherefore the Law was our schoolmaster to bring us unto Christ, that we might be justified by faith"—Galatians 3:24. The word for schoolmaster in Greek is "paidagogos," literally, "The one who leads the boy."

The Law of Moses has led us by the hand to Christ.

Only one who has lived under the Law and has come to know the liberating power of grace, may sing:

"Free from the law, O happy condition!
Jesus hath bled, and there is remission;
Cursed by the law and bruised by the fall,
Christ hath redeemed us once for all."